THINK
TO
WIN

THINK TO WIN

The Power of Logic in Everyday Life

S. CANNAVO, PH.D.

Prometheus Books

59 John Glenn Drive
Amherst, New York 14228-2197

Published 1998 by Prometheus Books

Inquiries should be addressed to
Prometheus Books
59 John Glenn Drive
Amherst, New York 14228–2197
VOICE: 716–691–0133, ext. 207
FAX: 716–564–2711
WWW.PROMETHEUSBOOKS.COM

07 06   7 6 5 4

Library of Congress Cataloging-in-Publication Data

Cannavo, S. (Salvator)
    Think to win : the power of logic in everyday life / S. Cannavo.
        p. cm.
    ISBN 1–57392–211–0 (alk. paper)
    1. Reasoning. I. Title.

BC177.C343 1998
160—dc21

98–12719

Printed in the United States of America on acid-free paper

ACKNOWLEDGMENTS

The students and colleagues from whom I have learned so much over the years while teaching philosophy and logic are more than I can name here. I thank them all and first.

I also wish to thank Queens College of the City University of New York for the opportunity to develop and teach "The Uses of Reason," in their cross-disciplinary program "Business Administration and the Liberal Arts." The strong emphasis which BALA placed on concrete applications did much to bring me closer to the practical.

My good friend Carl Heyel, editor and author of books on decision making, carefully read the entire text, getting so immersed as to come out of it ready for an honorary degree in practical logic. His many observations were invaluable.

But there are others to whom I am deeply indebted. The first of these is my literary agent, Alan Kellock, of the Kellock Company. He kept me going with unrelenting collegial effort and enthusiasm even when a serious back injury almost totally immobilized me for a year. His editorial acumen and his review comments jump-started the tightening process so necessary in making our subject more accessible to the general reader.

For their reading select chapters and offering helpful suggestions I thank Professors Stanley Malinovich in the Department of Philosophy at Brooklyn College of CUNY and Robert Karmon in the Department of English at Nassau Community College of SUNY. Finally, I cannot fail to thank my editor, Kathy Deyell of Prometheus Books. Her remarkably masterful editing and her insightful, substantive recommendations are what made possible the final product.

And now for those close by who had no choice but to put up with me for so long. I thank Peter, my son, for having enough reserve compassion to take pity and throw me a line when I SOS'd. Besides being my earliest critic, he miraculously deciphered and keyboarded the first inscrutable, hand-written draft just before hurrying off to his own graduate studies at Harvard. The dearest and closest of my benefactors, though, was my wife, Gaetana—a superb teacher and brilliant poet whose genius for nuance and compression made her constant input a sine qua non of my literary existence. But I owe her for much more. Without her unwavering encouragement and loving support, the writing of this book would have remained a mere fantasy.

CONTENTS

7

PART FOUR. IDEAS: CONCEPT SURGERY

HOW I CAME TO WRITE THIS BOOK

I owe the decision to write this book primarily to a former student, one of my very best, who popped into my office at the college one Friday afternoon. Francesca was now married and had mounted a few stress-rungs of the corporate ladder. She happened to be in the vicinity on business and stopped by to say hello.

Soon she asked with some disquiet if I could recommend a good book on how to think logically. She thought she really needed one. Too often at her department meetings, she knew the position she wanted to take—the position she thought was right —but couldn't formulate the convincing arguments that would get her there. She also longed to win more rounds with her husband, to pinpoint the fallacies she felt he sometimes committed in their discussions. Several of her friends complained of the same sort of thing. Would more reasoning have kept some of *them* out of the marital rapids they occasionally found themselves riding?

She went on to add that a few reasoning strategies would also be nifty at the local diner after the movies. With six or more people expressing opinions, the conversations tended to go in many directions at once, and that was okay, but it would be nice occasionally to focus things a bit more—to stay relevant and get to the bottom of some gnawing issue. She remembered how at one such gathering someone silenced her for the rest of the evening by accusing her of "begging the question." She was still not sure what he had meant.

But all of this was past or future. There was a real *present* problem—an urgent one. She was studying for her law exams (LSATs), and the logic questions on the practice sheets were impossible.

At this point, I handed Francesca one of our textbooks on reasoning, but she handed it right back. She didn't like text-books—too dry. She'd had enough of them in the past.

What she was asking for was a pleasing, leisurely reading experience that would walk her through the subject. Her hope was to pick up useful background—possibly some kind of orientation or "logical literacy" that could serve as a guide, especially in those critical situations that called for stand-up thinking. "But, no rules, no formulas, no diagrams, and please, no exercises!"

Was there such a book? Somewhat abashedly, I confessed I knew of none.

She was surprised. With all the books on how to *feel* better, weren't there any on how to *think* better? Doesn't thinking better also mean feeling better, especially about yourself? You *explain* better, *convince* better, *succeed* better—even appeal better as a woman or man.

"For God's sake, write one!" she said impatiently. "We can all use it."

As the disappointed young woman thanked me and left my office, she had no inkling of the impact her visit would have.

Minutes later, while driving home, her urgent mandate rang in my ears and I began to fashion a few of my own thoughts on reasoning as a subject for the general reader.

Our three children were home for spring break and dinner

talk that evening was a treat. The sentiment was unanimous. Wouldn't it be great to have something warm and engaging enough to hold any reader—something conversational and absolutely nonacademic, yet entirely true to the subject? "Really, Dad, all communicators could use it—students, parents, business managers. Even those of us in relationships."

I finally decided to start writing after I failed to find any book of the sort we had discussed. Store shelves that were brimming with tomes for putting us in touch with our feelings had nothing for putting us in touch with our thinking.

This book is a modest contribution toward filling that gap. Its aim is to acquaint the reader with those simple but hidden features of reasoning that make it the most empowering of human activities. I have attempted to offer a plain-language reading experience about *cogent* everyday thinking in *real* everyday contexts. To this effect, the examples in the discussion have been culled largely from the news, entertainment, friends, and personal experiences. The idea throughout has been to highlight the points of logic in the kind of everyday situations we can all relate to. Some of our examples therefore should and will ring very familiar to you.

The two payoffs of our reading journey are (1) an intimate, inside look at a most timely subject that—amazingly enough—has been kept under academic wraps since the beginning of educational time and (2) a raised logical consciousness that can serve as the lifelong guide to better reasoning.

Part One

HOW WE REASON:
The Anatomy of Argument

1

TO BEGIN WITH . . .

There are no educators. As a thinker one should speak only of
self-education.

Nietzsche, *Human All-too-Human* (267)

This book promises self-enlightenment. It is about reasoning—
the kind of thinking that best moves us toward the goals we
desire most. It offers reasoning as *the* alternative to New-Age
feel-good spiritualism, psychism, and post-science mysticism—
especially of the "quantum hocum" variety—all presently stacking the nation's bookshelves in diluvial quantities. Indulgence in
the swirls of such balm can seem sweet, but it cannot replace reasoning in any thrust at good living that has the slightest intention
of succeeding. And it certainly cannot replace the kind of
thinking that has taken us from blood-letting to antibiotics and
from the totem pole to the Internet.

REASONING AND FEELING

I don't mean to suggest, even for a moment, that mind and heart live apart and at odds with each other. Quite the opposite—our intellect and our feelings are intimately entwined. Reasoning not only dignifies what we feel, it also helps secure those feelings which, in the end, we always judge to have been most right for us. What I have in mind are feelings like personal fulfillment, self-confidence, and a good sense of who we are. These are feelings about ourselves, feelings we must have in order to live well, feelings we need as much as we need some of our most vital organs. And we all know from personal experience how reassuring, exhilarating, and gratifying it is when—with reasoned thought—we persuade someone (possibly even ourselves) or clear a mystery or come up with a great new idea. The ultimate winning card in all this is reasoning. It is the win–win mode of thinking by which all parties win honestly and with good reasons rather than by emotional dupery, or worse, by prevarication, deception, or subjection.

Pop counselors of every sort keep tracing ever more roads to better feelings about ourselves, but they say nothing about sound thinking as the master key to the *well-being* that is a necessary condition for the "real" good feelings. They must either be thinking we are all uniformly flawless in our reasoning with no need for further concern, or else they believe that though we may all differ in this capacity, we are essentially stuck with what is given us at birth. I'm convinced that both these assumptions are wrong. We can all benefit from greater awareness of what it is that makes reasoning work. And the rest of this book is my testimonial that this is so.

REASONING, BOTH NATURAL AND HUMAN

The capacity to reason distinguishes us dramatically from all other creatures. This is why Aristotle defined humans as reasoning animals and why anthropologists refer to us as *Homo sapiens*, which means "thinking man."

The activity of reasoning is familiar to all of us; we do it all the time and for all sorts of purposes. We reason when we argue over an issue like allowing sex education, when we justify having told a lie, when we figure out what must have caused the plane crash, or when we predict and change the course of a disease. We reason when we analyze and debate great ideas like 'freedom' or 'justice,' 'reasonable doubt' or 'love.' And we also reason, though in most cases haphazardly, when we come up with an idea no one else has ever had—like the first thought of an atom, a wheel, a supporting arch, a business strategy, or a new party game. We reason even in those wildly skeptical moments when we dare challenge the firmest beliefs—though in doing so, we may be seen as irreverent heretics or as egg-heads verging on madness. I am reminded here of the martyrdom, agonies, and disparagements endured by reasoning giants like Giordano Bruno whose "many worlds" hypothesis brought him death at the stake; Galileo, whose radical cosmology put him under the heel of the Inquisition; and Einstein, whose monumental and revolutionary theories were unthinkably dismissed by some as "Jewish science."

The human capacity to reason is the most impressive phenomenon on this planet and perhaps in the entire universe. And we're remarkably good at it, compared to all other creatures. When it comes to actual performance, though, we're hardly ever good enough. In a world which is stubbornly resistant, incurably competitive, and fueled by ever-expanding needs, we all inevitably run up against our intellectual limitations. We blunder repeatedly—at home, with friends, in the workplace—and the experience is always unbearably painful. When it comes to our intelligence, every occasion in which we're challenged seems crucial. Self-appraisal, social standing, personal future—all rolled up in one—seem to be on the firing line. And, alas, sometimes they really are. Or, at least, Steve, a consumer advocate, thought so one stomach-souring evening in a television studio.

The broadcast was on, and Steve was making some strong

remarks about drug prices: "Drug prices are the scandal of this decade. One hundred dollars a month for Zantac is outrageous no matter how well it works for stomach ulcers! And there are medications that cost many times more."

Carol, the drug industry representative, broke in: "Zantac too expensive? Try instead a round of duodenal surgery starting at twenty-five thousand—not to mention all the pain and risk."

This was an easy one for Steve as he proceeded to reduce Carol's claim to absurdity: "Well then, we should be paying hundreds of dollars for a toothbrush and a roll of dental floss. Without them cavities and gum disease would cost us thousands."

But Carol was not through yet: "You all know that drug research is very expensive and few projects ever succeed. One can never expect Glaxo or any other manufacturer to shoulder that kind of risk unless there is a real potential for profit. Restrict price and you throttle research, and also dim the hopes of those who are desperate for new remedies."

Steve sensed a flaw in this second argument, but this time he was silent too long. Cindy, the moderator, jumped in: "But you haven't shown us that Glaxo had to price Zantac *that* high. Possibly, the company could and would have taken the risk even if it had anticipated only half or even a quarter the present profits. How does one match price to risk in such cases?"

Steve left the studio still obsessing: "Darn it! As consumer advocate, I should have been the one to fire that last salvo. Sharp gal, that Cindy."

Clearly, Carol's slider was a fast one, but the pitch was seriously flawed. It rested on the arguable assumption that Glaxo would *not* have had the incentive to develop Zantac at a lower profit expectation. Her claim that Zantac, even at a high price, is better than surgery was, of course, true, but trivial and irrelevant. Certainly, Zantac at $2.50 per tablet is better than surgery at $25,000, but so is Zantac at $5 or $10 or $150 per tablet. Where does it stop? Carol was not supposed to justify choosing Zantac over surgery; to make an issue of *that* choice was only a distraction (logicians call this a "red herring"). What she should have been justifying, instead, was charging $2.50 over charging less. In offering only two alternatives, high price or surgery, she was deceptively presenting the panel with what is technically called a "false dilemma," i.e., an argument which ignores all but two usually extreme alternatives. (We will discuss fallacious moves of this sort later, in our sections on fallacies.)

Fortunately, the moderator promptly asked the "right" question, but it was too late for Steve.

> "Backward, turn backward, oh time in your flight."*
> I now have the answer I needed last night!

Okay, we're only human, not gods. So why not simply accept our fallibility? The best answer here seems to be a yes/no. Fallibility comes with being human, certainly, but it hardly follows that the less fallible we are the less human we are. We value our wit, not our drool. It's smart to be smarter. Not only is the personal payoff precious, but the overall stakes can be enormous!

THE POWER OF REASONING

We all know the power of reasoning, firsthand—what it can do when it is good and what it can cost us when it is bad. I'm sure you will recall striking examples of this in your own life and in what you've read of human history. I cannot resist mentioning an example that goes way back, one which, for its extraordinary elegance, i.e., combined simplicity and power, is virtually unmatched anywhere and any time in human history. The reasoner was Eratosthenes, a Greek librarian in Alexandria, 250 B.C.E. Reasoning at the level of today's high school junior, he actually computed the circumference of the earth to within fifty miles of the presently accepted value—all without ever leaving Alexandria and with only one tiny measurement. An astounding feat!

---

*Elizabeth A. Allen, "Rock Me to Sleep."

Here's how he did it. It all happened one day in Alexandria about 250 B.C.E. Eratosthenes knew from experience that at noon on June 21 (the summer solstice), the sun over Syene would shine directly overhead. Also from experience, he knew that this would not be the case in Alexandria, which was 500 miles directly north of Syene and which he therefore assumed was on the same meridian (line of longitude) as Syene. So on June 21 at noon in Alexandria, he measured the angle "between" the sun's rays and a vertical pole. The rest was a simple arithmetical proportion which even a teenager can handle. (For a brief sketch of this simple computation, consult the *Encyclopedia Britannica* under "Eratosthenes" and "Geodesy.")

Unfortunately, someone else reasoning badly later determined the number to be one-third this value, and, later still, others, again reasoning badly, accepted the erroneous number as the correct value. Because of these two errors, Columbus, seventeen centuries later, thought he had reached the Orient, or possibly the shores of India, after crossing only three thousand miles of ocean!

CAN WE BE SMARTER?

Neurobiologists tell us that thinking is not simply the unfathomable activity of an abstractly structured and preformed "mind" —a mind presumably fixed for life by the hard wiring we're born with. What they talk about, instead, is the *plasticity* of vast neural networks in the brain that undergo measurable changes as we learn and remember. More specifically, these are changes in "connectivity," a property of neural networks that measures the ease with which they fire and that neuroscientists think corresponds to our acquired skills and cognitive capabilities. It is observed that the more often the neural pathways involved are used, the more easily they fire. The connectivity of select neural networks, therefore, is demonstrably heightened with use.

Pondering the several hundred billion neurons that are networking and re-networking in the brain, researchers are now saying that no one yet knows what limits there are to what the human brain can be or do. Their efforts, it seems, still have not yielded any clues as to where to set such boundaries. Can it be, then, that inherent in the human intellect is a reserve potential for cognitive development that is practically without bottom?

We must add to this hardware potential the incredibly empowering tool we call language, namely, words and the concepts we associate with them. These are the finest and most incisive tools of the mind, the prosthetic devices which vastly multiply and extend our mental reach, and infuse the world around us with human intelligence. Early in life, we learn to use words with breath-taking speed. Sentences and reasoning soon follow. In this sense, intelligence is learned and the learning need never stop!

These neurological and linguistic perspectives on learning are certainly exciting, but the entire history of education is equally compelling. Our teachers for the past two thousand years have all assumed that studying any subject improves our cognitive skills, i.e., makes us smarter—at least in that subject. And no one since the beginning has ever really succeeded in falsifying this proposition. The underlying analogy is crude but straightforward enough. If physical exercise strengthens the body, then why shouldn't mental exercise do the same for the mind? This working hypothesis is of long enough standing to merit assigning it at least a good measure of plausibility. It would seem, at any rate, that if it were false, much of general education since the beginning would have been one grotesque delusion.

THE STUDY OF REASONING:
Reasoning about Reasoning

Okay then, what about studying reasoning itself as a subject in its own right? Shouldn't we be zeroing in on the principles that make it work so "miraculously," that give it its "correctness"? What better way can there be of sharpening our thinking?

The astounding fact is that until only a few decades ago,

schools never offered courses in *reasoning*. Even now, it is *sujet perdu* except in some philosophy departments. Ironically, though all our teachers urge us to think correctly, they leave us in the dark about precisely what makes thinking right or wrong. Reasoning, as it were, never made it as a "fourth R" alongside reading, 'riting, and 'rithmetic. Putting this more pointedly, our schools leave us illiterate on the principles of sound reasoning, forever depriving us of the surest way to self-monitor and self-improve our thinking. This is a gap that can follow us throughout life no matter how accomplished we become.

What we're after, therefore, is logical literacy or awareness of basics. The clearest evidence of logic's importance comes from those who teach elementary reasoning and critical thinking in our colleges. These observers report that their students show dramatic improvement across the whole curriculum, not only on routine examinations but also, and especially, in written and oral expression. My own experience in teaching reasoning to undergraduates corroborates these results. The improvement is almost incredible, especially in their writing. It starts to blossom as soon as they become aware of what to look for in order to distinguish between sound and flawed thinking.

Should any of this be so surprising? Isn't it helpful in the learning of many skills to be aware of the underlying basics? Labor leaders, politicians, business executives, sales representatives, and actors, for example, those who, with practice, may become effective speakers, are willing to pay substantial fees for seminars in public speaking. These courses do more than simply provide more practice. They acquaint students with the principles of effective communication and guide them on how to apply these in actual speech-making. It is in this way rather than by blind skill and drill methods (through rote memorization and repetition) that such courses make possible later self-monitoring and self-improvement.

Reasoning seems to be a particularly good candidate for benefiting from a study of this sort. As we'll go on to see, the earmarks of good reasoning are easily identified and remembered. Incredible though it may seem, the fundamental principles are very few and very simple, so that assimilating them for the guidance of thought is anything but difficult. (If it were up to me, I would introduce some of these as early as the fourth grade.) Even a brief and casual introduction to the subject can engender a significant measure of logical awareness. The rest, then, is a matter of implementing this awareness in the lifelong process of self-correction.

The potential for continual "logical growth" is limitless. We reason almost constantly, even at the most elementary levels of activity, and this means we have on-going opportunity for utilizing whatever techniques and insights we acquire. Meaningful practice, therefore, is unavoidable, and the successes which we rake up will provide reinforcement for more successes.

THE THREE OBJECTIVES OF THIS BOOK

Our first and main objective is to spark the kind of logical awareness or orientation that will serve as a lifelong guide to effective thinking. To heighten this orientation, we will look closely not only at good reasoning but also at certain standard kinds of bad reasoning called fallacies. We all commit these to an extent that is nothing short of epidemic, and when our leaders, bureaucrats, managers, and even experts do it with impunity, the consequences can be and sometimes are disastrous. Getting to recognize and screen for fallacies, therefore, is a giant step in our consciousness-raising objective.

Our second aim is to present reasoning not as another school discipline, but as a subject of general interest. My basic conviction here is that each of us, at all places and levels of activity, has, over and over again, felt the compelling magic of effective thinking. If I'm right about this, there is in every one of us a latent curiosity about what it is that gives reasoning its awesome power—its power to move us through the darkness of mystery, prejudice, and conflict, and toward something we can reasonably call "true."

To arouse this curiosity fully and then go on to address it, we need only open an inviting doorway to the intriguing configurations in our daily logic—configurations which only humans can construct. Our discussion, therefore, aims to be intimate, informal, and illustrated with day-to-day situations that are deliberately simple so as to reveal the underlying logic. The idea is to unravel for the non-student the one important subject that is still a shadowy trade secret of the academy, and has been so since the very first teacher walked with a student. Locked within the hard covers of textbooks, this most universal of all subjects—the one that applies to all things and is perhaps the most human of the humanities—has remained largely inaccessible to the general reader and uncultivated in our daily existence.

It was Emerson who first introduced the concept of *self-culture*, but he did so only as a means for the self-development of what he called "spiritual vision." I would broaden this concept to include the cultivation of logical principle as a means for the self-development of rational intelligence.

This book is an invitation to don our walking shoes—not our academic stilts—and to stroll through the back-ways of day-to-day reasoning. The idea is to do it not in any cut-and-dried textbook manner, but naturally and conversationally all the way. No daunting exercises to distract us, nothing for us to memorize, and no dead formulas to autopsy.

Our third and final objective is an aesthetic one. Reasoning and the understanding which usually follows can be deeply satisfying—just remember how we all feel when the "light goes on." And what about the challenge of the process itself? Mysteries and puzzles have been fun and games since the beginning of human time. I've heard even children say of some well-structured argument that it was "neat" or "cool." They could only have meant by this that there was something intensely pleasing about it. All good reasoning is appealing in this way. It puts order, purpose, and value in the chaotic stream we call thinking.

The third of our aims, then, is to highlight the aesthetic in logical order or structure. Doing so is bound to brighten our appreciation of it and the pleasure we quite naturally take in it. Better living and a better world is justification enough for better reasoning, but enhancing the unique pleasure and satisfaction it offers—not to mention the sense of power—can help make it a first-choice modality in our lives. And by the way, if reasoning is almost always pleasurable, then consider reasoning about reasoning and understanding how we understand: How pleasurable might these be?

*   *   *

Now that you've stayed the distance through these broad scoutings and ambitious comments about our subject and aims, we go to the next chapter to start our main voyage. There, we'll ask, What exactly *is* reasoning? What kinds of reasoning are there, and how do they work?

2

REASONS:
Justifying Our Claims

STUDENT: Prove to me, sir, that logic is useful.

EPICTETUS: Yes, but tell me first how I could ever do such a thing without using logic.

(ca. C.E. 100)

WE ALL REASON—But How?

Reasoning is something we're all familiar with. It starts spontaneously, early in life, the moment we try to make some sense of our surroundings or when someone first asks us why we believe that something is so. After that our ability to reason grows rapidly as we exercise it more and more in one situation after another. Little wonder no school ever offered us a course in reasoning: This capacity comes to us early and naturally.

As adults we reason almost constantly, usually without being aware of it or noticing how we do it. Because of this, our reasoning is largely informal and to some extent even haphazard. But wow, how it wins! And it wins in a very special way. It wins by convincing rather than by defeating, and by informing rather than by deceiving.

We all reason, we're good at it, and it gets us through most of the chaos and challenges of daily life. But—and here is the rock-bottom assumption throughout this book—by becoming more aware of *how* we reason we can tap more deeply into this largely human power. Who wouldn't want to fare better with one's boss, colleagues, friends, adversaries, children, lover—and even with oneself?

All reasoning is, of course, thinking, but *not* all thinking is reasoning. I'm thinking but not reasoning when I *recall* how my mother smiled in her radiant days, or when I *hope* to get well, or *resolve* never to take another drink, or when I suddenly *see* the beauty of a line in a familiar poem. Even when I simply express a belief I am not reasoning. I can, for example claim that one way to reduce violent crime is to reduce poverty. But I am just thinking, not reasoning, if I make no attempt to *justify* or defend this claim. I can of course make some such attempt, i.e., give "reasons" for my claim, as for example, by citing the deprivation, frustration, and antisocial anger that go with poverty and lead to violence. As soon as I do this, I am no longer just thinking; I'm reasoning.

ARGUMENTS

Consider another simple example of reasoning:

> Although manatees live in water, they are mammals, because manatees suckle their young and only mammals do that sort of thing.

The point is by now obvious. Reasoning consists of offering reasons in support of a claim. Logicians call the reasons *premises* and the claim they support a *conclusion*. The premises plus the conclusion they call an *argument*, and we, ourselves, will follow this jargon.

Our argument about manatees can now be summarized in the following way:

CLAIM (CONCLUSION):

• Manatees are mammals.

REASONS (PREMISES):

• Manatees suckle their young.
• Only mammals do that sort of thing.

Clearly, we're not using the term "argument" here to refer to squabbles, as we often do in everyday contexts. Of course, even in our most heated disagreements there will be traces of reasoning. In such a case, however, it is only the reasoned portions that we will regard as arguments and nothing else. In saying this, I blush as I recall how my wife warns that "the loud sounds" I sometimes make when I disagree with her will never convince her. Only reasons will.

COMPELLING CONNECTIONS

What is it, then, that gives an argument its power? Why argue (give reasons) for any of our claims?

For one thing, reasons get your foot in the door. Anyone who buys into your reasons is agreeing that they are, in some sense, applicable. Such a customer is therefore, to some extent, obliged to accept your claim or else face the charge of being unreasonable, and this is a charge he doesn't easily live down once it sticks. Ignorance is not so bad; it is only a temporary affliction. Unreasonableness, on the other hand, is seen as a chronic condition.

But reasons are more than rhetoric for generating a vague sense of obligation. Often, they genuinely convince the listener. For instance, recall our example about manatees: If we know that manatees suckle their young and that only mammals do that (our premises), we must also grant that manatees are mammals (our conclusion). We might want to conclude, also, that manatees are not fish, assuming of course that if something is a fish, it cannot also be a mammal. Setting this additional reasoning aside, the move from premises to conclusion in our main argument is *absolutely* compelling.

In our first example about poverty, the argument is less compelling, but even there, there is some convincing power. The power in both arguments obviously lies in the connection between reasons and conclusion—a connection by virtue of which the conclusion more or less "follows" from the premises. This connection is entirely absent from the cliché jingle:

> Roses are red, violets are blue.
> I am, therefore, in love with you.

but to some extent present in:

> Roses are red, but I prefer blue.
> So send me some violets with no further ado.

So far, we have said very little about what connects premises or reasons to a conclusion in an argument. We have exhibited the connection in two very simple examples and have described the resulting arguments as more or less compelling. Our root question, however, remains: How does this connection work? How do arguments vary in their power to convince? Can it be that there are two fundamentally different kinds of them?

TWO BASIC KINDS OF ARGUMENTS

We all know that some arguments are more compelling than others. Eyewitness reports, for example, will lend a prosecutor's argument (case) much more strength than the results of a DNA test. But some arguments are not just very strong, they're strong in a very special sense.

Consider the argument:

> *(Premises)*   All HIV infections are fatal.
>   Smith's is an HIV infection.
>   *Therefore*
> *(Conclusion)*   Smith's infection is fatal.

This is an elementary and, some might say trivial, argument, but it does represent one of the standard logical forms and its simplicity serves our purposes. What we want to notice about the argument is something more than that the reasons or premises support the conclusion. They do so in an *entirely conclusive* way. (Our argument about manatees is exactly of this kind.) If all HIV infections are in fact fatal (and maybe they're not) and if Smith's is an HIV infection, then, necessarily, Smith's infection is fatal. This conclusion follows absolutely and inescapably from its premises. Putting it a little differently, in this argument it simply is not possible for the premises to be true and the conclusion false.

We should bear firmly in mind here that we're not asking whether the premises of these arguments are themselves true. Are, in fact, all HIV infections fatal? Does Smith actually have HIV? For the moment, these questions are entirely beside the point. What we are saying is that in this argument (as in the one about manatees) there is a positively and perfectly tight connection between the reasons and the conclusion. This is what is known as the *deductive* relationship which, in many cases, we are often able to sense immediately without ever having had any training in logic. Logicians call the arguments which feature this relationship *deductive arguments*. In chapter 13, where we revisit deduction for a really close look, we will discover why the deductive connection is so absolutely compelling.

Now, let's change our HIV example just a bit:

(Premises)	*Nearly* all HIV infections are fatal.
	And Smith's is an HIV infection.
	Therefore (Probably)
(Conclusion)	Smith's infection is fatal.

This second argument, like the first, is strong, but it is fundamentally different from its predecessor. Its reasons or premises do *not* fully guarantee its conclusion. They support it, but the support is limited. Yes, it would be grossly unreasonable to conclude that Smith's infection is not fatal once we accept the premises, but such a conclusion would be entirely consistent with those premises. It certainly could be true that nearly all HIV infections are fatal and that Smith's particular one is not. Following most logicians, we will classify arguments of this sort as *nondeductive* or simply as *inductive* arguments.

Inductive arguments make up the major portion of our day-to-day reasoning and we'll take a much closer look at them in part three, where we'll see that inductive reasoning can take several basic forms—one of which, characterized as *diagnostic,* calls for a very creative and incisive kind of thinking.

*   *   *

We have just viewed the most general structure of arguments:

Argument = premises + conclusion

But can it be all that simple? Yes, essentially, except for a few important qualifications and precautions. So let's step into our next chapter for a view of these.

3

CAVEAT EMPTOR:
Look Before You Leap

HIDDEN ASSUMPTIONS

Reasoning is often far less transparent than the tidy examples we have considered so far. Imagine a man missing his wallet shortly after returning home from the local bank. The endless and frantic search is on, and he asks his wife if she's seen it.

HE: Where is it? I've looked everywhere for nearly half an hour. I must have missed the inside pocket of my jacket and dropped it. The floor at the bank is carpeted; there was no thud.

SHE: No, if you had dropped it, someone would surely have seen it and turned it in. By this time, the bank would have called. Your ID and phone number were in the wallet. Besides, you had very little money in it. Look some more. It's got to be in the house somewhere.

HE: I had better go to the Department of Motor Vehicles for a duplicate driver's license. Whoever found my wallet kept it.

Here we have two reasoners. Both are answering the same question, on the basis of the same factual information, within practically the same context, but they arrive at different conclusions and are each poised for very different kinds of action. The reason is simply the difference in what they're assuming but not stating. She assumes that the people in the neighborhood are conscientious enough to return the wallet, especially when personal documents are involved. He, on the other hand, assumes the opposite. To unlock the disagreement we must identify and expose these hidden assumptions. Obviously, it is only after this has been done that the uncovered assumptions can be properly evaluated. Agreement on some factual basis then becomes more likely. This example is of course of little or no lifetime consequence, and may therefore seem somewhat trivial. It is representative, however, of a huge portion of our day-to-day, time-thieving bickerings. Its simplicity also serves to highlight the point of logic involved.

Hidden assumptions can delay resolving personal issues especially when, sometimes out of reluctance to have our underlying beliefs challenged or tested, we blot them even from our own awareness. My wife, for years, remained firmly convinced that air travel was the most dangerous sport around. She gave all sorts of other reasons for not wanting to vacation overseas: the bad taste of foreign water, malaria, sleeping sickness, hepatitis, mad-cow disease, keeping one's tourist money in the American economy, and, finally, even the coziness of cars and trains or the unequaled beauty of our local scenery. Relevant though these reasons may have been, her argument would have been much more transparent if she had also included what she believed about the dangers of air travel. When she finally saw how real her fear of flying was, she expressed it explicitly and became, therefore, able to engage in some meaningful discussion about it. We are no longer grounded. She now flies willingly, though perhaps not without apprehension.

Implicit assumptions are sometimes made as oversights, and these can be costly. I may, for example, argue in favor of opting for the lowest estimate rather than the fastest job in the replacement of our cesspool. In doing so, however, I am implicitly and perhaps naively assuming that whoever does the job will do the work honestly and reliably anyway. My stated reasons will be only about the advantages of low cost over early completion. Again, in recently choosing a contractor to do our driveway, I chose the lowest bid, unwittingly assuming that all driveway asphalt is of about the same granular mix. Had I not made this unfortunate assumption, I could have opted for a finer mix than the one we got, even though this would have cost more.

These examples were chosen because they are simple and transparent for the sake of the point. Where the reasoning is more complex, however, implicit assumptions can cause more serious delays. A few years ago, prior to the Desert Storm War in Iraq in 1991, the following paraphrased comment was made on the House of Representatives floor while the United Nations was imposing sanctions on Iraq in order to force a withdrawal from Kuwait:

> No one wants war. We all dread its casualties even when we wage it against a cruel and dangerous despot. I have pondered the question of direct military action for several months through many sleepless nights, and the way to go seems perfectly clear. We cannot let Saddam Hussein reap profit from his aggression, nor can we allow a hostile dictator to harass the world economy by letting him keep his ill-gotten oil fields in Kuwait. Negotiation is out of the question because it would entail rewarding him with concessions for his aggression. Finally, while we hesitate to take decisive action, he continues to dig in near the Kuwait border. War soon will be costly. War later will be more costly.

In this argument the author's conclusion is, obviously, that we should go to war with Iraq at once. (He never quite states this explicitly but he strongly implies it.) The reasons or justifications he gives are that we cannot allow Hussein to reap profit from his aggression; that we cannot allow him to harass the world economy with his grip on oil; that we ought not negotiate and risk having to make concessions; and that in time Hussein will entrench himself near the Kuwait border so that war later will be more costly than war now. The author of this argument, however, assumes—without saying so—that sanctions would not work acceptably soon enough.

What is most remarkable about this entire episode is the time it took to expose the assumption. After much boggling about the price of a hot war and about which nations should shoulder the military burden, one congressman finally singled out and challenged the speaker's hidden assumption.

By now you may quite rightly be wondering whether all the implicit assumptions we make when we reason should be ruthlessly ferreted out and displayed for the sake of clarity. The answer must of course be no, and here's why.

A very good reason for not stating an assumption is the author's belief that everyone accepts the assumption as true. By far, most of our implicit assumptions are of this sort. I may argue, for instance, that inflation will continue to stay down for the rest of the year, giving as solid reasons that the government reports a cooling economy and rising inventories. In arguing this way, I am assuming without saying so that in the meantime there will not be a global calamity such as a major war or a collision with some huge asteroid. I don't bother stating this assumption simply because I believe anybody would grant it as true or at least as highly probable.

The same kind of exemptions apply to the wallet owner's reasoning. He assumes, for example, that banks, unlike some restaurant kitchens, are not places where a hungry rodent is apt to run off with the wallet for its tasty leather. He also assumes that the net force on the wallet, had it slipped past his coat, is that of gravity—straight down rather than upward or sideways. It therefore could not have landed in a wastepaper basket or flown out an open window. He also makes many other assumptions which express basic things he knows and thinks everybody else knows.

Only a moment's reflection tells us that virtually all our reasoning is similarly supported in part by countless assumptions.

These assumptions are drawn from a vast pool of shared beliefs so well established as to be accepted as basic knowledge by all concerned. Even in the "hard" sciences key assumptions are implicitly made by the handful. Every experiment presupposes all sorts of things about laboratory instruments, about certain uniformities in nature, about how much we disturb subject matter the moment we observe it, even about human perception itself and the fidelity with which it mirrors external "reality." Does this mean we never challenge generally accepted assumptions, especially those made at the most hallowed levels of human knowledge? Again, no!

The most stunning advances in the history of science have been made when a daredevil thinker has challenged some belief implicitly held by the scientific community for hundreds and even thousands of years. I cannot resist recalling some age-old assumptions that have, at one time or another, been challenged and defeated in this way, thereby sparking a revolution in the going scientific view of the world around us. Here are a few:

- The earth is the center of the universe.
- Freely moving bodies eventually come to a stop, even in the absence of friction.
- Every object is either absolutely at rest or absolutely in motion.
- The flow and exchange of energy is always smooth and continuous.
- Light in a perfect vacuum travels in perfectly straight lines.
- The motion of an object has no effect on its mass or its dimensions.
- Time flows the same way for all observers, no matter how they're moving.
- In principle, we can always make corrections for any disturbances we cause in a system whenever we observe it.
- The ubiquitous vacuum in the universe is "pure," "empty" space, incapable, by itself, of giving rise to any new material entity.

- If we keep shortening the tails of mice generation after generation after generation, they will eventually be born with shorter tails.

And the list can be made a lot longer.

Here is an amusing example of how blindly "assuming" we can sometimes be: A friend of mine once visited his aunt in Grand Forks, North Dakota, after not having been there in three and a half years. When he was served coffee, he remarked that the coffee somehow tasted different. "Oh," said his aunt, "how can that be? It came from the very same can I used the last time you were here. You see, we ourselves really don't drink much coffee."

IMPLICIT VALUE ASSUMPTIONS:
The Inevitable Clash and Incendiary Mixture

Okay, seemingly irreconcilable disagreement between reasoning parties can often be resolved. This is especially so when the disagreement is rooted in arguable assumptions that, once exposed, can be factually tested and perhaps decided upon.

Unfortunately, however, resolving a disagreement is not always a matter of simply determining what the "facts" are. Even after all assumptions have been exposed and examined, some of them may not be matters of fact at all. They may reflect, instead, the values—ethical orientations, aesthetic preferences, and personal interests—of those who make them. What, for example, is more precious: the opportunities which a free market offers or the overall security of a highly planned and controlled economy? Imagine the hopelessness of trying to reach agreement if two individuals argue from different starting points on this issue, especially if the answers they assume are wholly or even partially hidden. As a start, at least, it is therefore important to recognize those cases of disagreement in which heavy value clashes rather than merely factual ones are involved.

Unfortunately, a major portion of human disagreement stems from value rather than factual differences, and these can be stubbornly resistant to reconciliation. Budget deadlocks in government, for example, are often not about whether or not balancing would improve the economy. This is ordinarily a factual issue, and many (though not all) agree it should and can be done. The disagreement usually is on how to do it, on which programs to trim: the military, foreign aid, environment, welfare, education, etc.? This is a value-laden issue, a matter of priorities and interests, and not simply a matter of facts.

Here is the gist of a recent dispute in one of my classes over another vital issue. The clash of underlying values in this exchange is obvious.

> Abortion is the destruction of life—the killing of a potential human being. It is brutalizing and should be illegal at any time.

> Depriving a woman of choice, especially in the first trimester of pregnancy, amounts to depriving her of sovereignty over her own body. When we do this we extinguish the deepest core of her personhood, namely, her autonomy and therefore her dignity. This is a crushing and dispiriting coercion imposed on a *real* person. It is a far more brutalizing form of "killing" than the interruption of a process that offers only the biological *potential* for producing a future person.

It seems highly unlikely that either side in these issues would ever accept the position of the other, but recognizing where the clash is and that it is one of values rather than facts can be critically effective in moving the disputants toward a reasonable compromise in the search for some common ground.

I should mention, in passing, a practice that is probably as common as the padding of deductibles on tax returns. This is the roguish art of using unsubstantiated factual claims to support some value-laden position on a major issue. Let me illustrate by paraphrasing a debate I recently heard at an education forum:

We should provide condoms. Our schoolchildren will have sex anyway, with or without them. We can, of course, strongly advise abstinence, but we can also impress on them that if they don't use the condoms, they can become pregnant or fatally ill. Though these devices do occasionally fail, their failure rate is relatively low and not prohibitive. Their use can therefore yield a significant drop in unwanted pregnancies and venereal infection.

I oppose distributing condoms to school children. It grotesquely contradicts the recommendation to abstain and would actually encourage greater sexual activity. Children are naturally careless about using such devices, and their failure rate is high. The net effect would be that of exposing children to more danger than ever before.

In this dialogue the speakers make confident, matter-of-fact pronouncements about the effectiveness of condoms and about how much sex children will have with or without them. What is important to note, however, is that these speakers take wide liberties by offering unsupported and arguable, factual statements as though they are established truths. Actually, neither the debaters nor their audiences are, at the time of discussion, in a position to test or even ring up any significant support for these claims.

This kind of "fact mongering" is a powerful and frequently used ensnaring technique. When you encounter it look for strong, underlying value orientations. Our first speaker may be more concerned than the second with averting the dangers of teenage sexual activity and somewhat less concerned with abstaining. The second, on the other hand, may be attaching greater significance to the act itself—and therefore to abstention—and less to consequences. It would surely help to clear the air on this. Someone might ask how the speakers feel about teenage sexual activity itself, quite apart from its physical and social consequences.

In discussions of this sort, the reasoners typically present their opinions as well established facts instead of thin likelihoods or even mere possibilities. Often they buttress their claims with arguable statistics—sometimes, even fictitious ones. The result is a mishmash of conflicting factual claims, the kind that so often confront us when we hear politicians or commentators debating an issue. In listening to the rhetoric in these cases, one usually cannot tell what is in fact true. This sort of thing may happen even in allegedly high-level discussions such as CNN's program *Crossfire*.

A VERY SERIOUS PROBLEM:
Separating Fact from Value

We've argued for separating factual from value issues in dealing with disagreement. It would seem, therefore, that doing this can simply be made a routine part of all rational discourse. Unfortunately this is not the way things are. There is a stumbling block, a big one, and it can make issues gummier than raw dough.

Suppose, for example, that a clinical trial is proposed whose objective is to test an antibody that has been genetically engineered for a rare but fatal form of cancer. The experiment can, possibly, establish a cure. There are, however, strong opponents of the project who claim that the possible benefits to a relatively small number of people do not justify the very high cost. How, in this case, does one begin to balance human lives against dollars? In offering their cost-benefit analysis, aren't the opponents felicitously assuming that we can somehow assign a dollar value to a single human life and, from there, to countless others in the future?

One way of making such a dollar assignment would be to canvass public opinion—but then, whom do we ask? Do we canvass the citizens at large or those who have the illness? If we do both, how do we weight the answers? Is the opinion of a healthy eighteen-year-old equivalent to that of a vulnerable "sixty-fiver" or of someone who is already terminally ill with the disease? We may choose the one-person, one-vote route which most of us would probably think impeccably fair, but wouldn't this also be just another value preference over other ways of counting?

In this last example, we started with what seemed to be a genuinely factual assumption, namely, that the dollar value of human life can somehow be determined, even if only approximately. Once we began reflecting on the assumption, however, we found ourselves enmeshed in a maze of value issues. Was the assumption, therefore, a matter of fact or of value?

HUMAN AFFAIRS AND THE FACT–VALUE TANGLE

When it comes to human affairs, separating facts from values can be a monumental task often leaving us with a sense of hopelessness and frustration, and it's not very hard to see why. Most basic to any social issue is the seemingly factual one of how badly people want some particular thing or "good." We must know this in order to balance the cost of that good against its benefit. But then, do we ask the citizens at large or the consumers of that good? Are we trapped here in a thick moral dilemma? Can we ever decide between public and special interests on value-neutral (i.e., factual) grounds?

One would think that the social sciences can marshall the methodical know-how for escaping the fact–value tangle. But we all know how the pundits sometimes disagree sharply on psychological, sociological, and political issues even when these appear to be strictly factual matters such as how to reduce crime, blunt discrimination, or improve education. The modern science of economics, even at its quantitative best, harbors rampant disagreements at the highest levels of expertise and on the most urgent issues such as poverty, the economy, and health care.

The quagmires in these cases are value differences. The assumptions may seem factual, but try to justify them and you are hopelessly stuck. Which sources of information do you go to? (Values!) Do you consult liberal or conservative texts? (Values!) Whom do you believe when the top experts disagree? (Values!) And how about those who get to do the research? What kinds of studies and experiments do they set up? (Values!) How do they weight the different strands of evidence? (Values!) And can they really interpret their results neutrally?

The fundamental difficulties we have just outlined are serious, and at the very least, they are strong reminders against oversimplification. But to throw up our hands and scotch the fact–value distinction altogether would, in day-to-day practice, be nothing short of reckless. In more ordinary affairs, we can often (usefully) agree on how to go about settling many differences by accepted factual methods. We can then try to sharpen and negotiate the value-residue. Looking to separate fact from value can still be very useful, though accomplishing the separation may be difficult and, in final analysis, necessarily incomplete. Even in more complex human affairs, the utility of holding to this critical distinction remains incalculable. The price of ignoring it can be endless controversy, frustration, and possibly cataclysmic conflict.

WORD TANGLES: Semantics

Our full understanding of any line of reasoning calls for exposing all *arguable* hidden assumptions, whether of the factual or value sort. It also opens the door to resolving those disagreements that are rooted in conflicting, unstated assumptions.

There is, however, yet another factor that can gridlock any discussion, and this is semantics. Are key words being used in the same way? If not, discussion can be about as productive as hole-punching in water. Let us look in on our two friends locked again in disagreement over abortion:

> I think a woman in the first trimester of pregnancy ought to have the right to choose abortion. After all, the basic consideration is that if she loses sovereignty of her own body during this period, she suffers an emotional "death" far more grievous than the early death of a fetus.

Not so! Her bodily sovereignty is not the only consideration. She may have the right to rule over her own body, but certainly not over the body of another individual. If she interrupts her pregnancy at any time, she terminates an innocent human life. And this violates the spirit of our laws which prohibit homicide. We ought to pass laws that protect *all* humans, born and unborn.

But how do you jump so quickly to homicide? A three-month-old fetus is certainly alive as is the skin on my nose. But I have trouble calling it an "individual" or an innocent human in the same sense in which we apply such terms to a three-month-old baby.

These two friends are certainly far apart on abortion and choice, but how they use words like "individual," "human," "life," "homicide," and even "innocent" tends to deepen the chasm between them. They are obviously not understanding these terms in quite the same way.

Clearing semantic underbrush of this sort seems necessary in any move toward agreement. In any argument, the ways in which we understand key words amount to unstated assumptions. We often assume word meanings without saying so in much of our reasoning. Such *semantic* assumptions are generally grantable as matters of common usage, and usually there is no need for announcements. Occasionally, however, a word used too loosely or in too special a sense is important enough in a discussion to cause sizable misunderstandings. Detecting the discrepancy, however, is often all we need for the occasion.

In a reported debate on whether chimpanzees are really using language when they communicate with their trainers, the disagreement seemed to be as much about words as about facts. The trainers maintained that the "chimp talk" they observed was an instance of language. Others denied that the chimps were using language. Fortunately, they eventually addressed the semantic issue of what it means to say that someone is "using language," and they observed that it means a lot more than merely associating things with words or symbols. It means constructing sentences of arbitrary length and complexity on the basis of rules which linguists call a "generative grammar" and which humans understand and apply easily. Now, were the chimps in the study doing anything at all like this? At any rate, it seems evident that closing the semantic gap between these disputants can go some of the way toward settling the more substantive matter of just what the chimps in the study were really doing.*

HIDDEN AGENDAS: Are They Part of Arguments?

If you're weighing the *strength* of some piece of reasoning—a business analysis, a reasoned High Court decision, a defense attorney's argument—do not look for agendas. Agendas are plans of action, purposes, objectives; they are not assumptions. They may be realistic or not, attainable or not, but they are not claims at all and therefore cannot possibly be assumptions. Nor, for these reasons, can they be conclusions. They are therefore not part of any argument. This means that hidden agendas are to be sharply distinguished from hidden assumptions, though the two may be easily confused. This whole book, for example, is in a broad sense an argument. One of my agendas (purposes) for writing it is to convince you that becoming familiar with how the process of logic works is both pleasing and practical. This agenda or purpose of mine, however, is not part of the argument.

To remain clear about any line of reasoning, therefore, keep out of consideration the hidden agendas that you suspect are "behind" the reasoning. If there is an agenda, it is motivational or psychological but not part of the logic itself. The reasoner's agenda tells you why the reasoner is engaging you with her reasoning in the first place. The answer is usually a very natural one: She simply wants to convince you of her conclusion. Why she wants to do this is an altogether different matter.

---

*"Chimp Talk Debate: Is It Really Language?" *New York Times,* June 6, 1995, p. C1.

What if the reasoning is preposterous or just remarkably unconvincing? In such a case, you would naturally want to know why. What on earth could be causing the reasoner to persist in a certain conclusion when his argument for it is so feeble? The idea, then, is not to clarify the reasoning or to resolve some reasoned difference, but to discover a cause of unreasonable thinking. Okay, it is then that we properly look for agendas.

The wife of the wallet owner implicitly assumes that the clients of the neighborhood bank are, for the most part, altruistic enough to turn in the wallets they find. This assumption is a dubious one and may in fact be false. Making it uncritically therefore flaws her reasoning. Why, then, does she embrace it so tightly? Does her particular personal experience support the all-trusting belief—a belief she may think most others hold? More likely, she is less clearly aware of exactly what she thinks, and here, an agenda (of sorts) enters the picture. She may, for example, need to manage the stress of the loss and get some sleep that night—and such an agenda can be so "hidden" that she, herself, is unaware of it.

PACKAGING AN ARGUMENT

I'm sure that most of the reasoned texts which you have seen have also contained portions that were neither premises nor conclusions. I am referring here to introductory background accounts, interesting anecdotes, illustrative examples, humor, sarcasm, nuances, threats, or, for that matter, any material that has no direct logical bearing on the author's conclusion. Some writers dismiss such portions of the text as irrelevant and refer to them as filler, padding, or even just fluff. Mostly they're just that: peripheral content which does not figure centrally in the main line of reasoning.

Don't knock peripheral content too hard, however. These characterizations are much too negative. Milder terms like "packaging," "embellishment," or "dressing" seem more in line with the fact that such auxiliary material can add to both the content and the clarity of the text. Obviously, the way we package an argument can highlight key points in the reasoning and give communicative life to the otherwise cold and winding pathways of argumentation. But packaging generally does more than direct our attention. It builds context, a factor that figures heavily in "fixing" the sense of what is being said.

Good communicators know this and employ embellishments skillfully. Others often fail miserably. How many times did your mind wander as some pedant droned on with his ifs, ands, and therefores? What a difference a few interesting asides, a few examples, or even some emotional gestures could have made!

Such devices do more than just keep you awake. They are major clues to a speaker's point of view and, therefore, to what she means by her words. In discussing the problem of poverty and malnutrition in the world, a representative from Somalia would probably mean something considerably different by the word "poor" than what an American might have in mind. Proper introductions and background embellishments make possible the conceptual and semantic "tunings" necessary for effective, high-resolution communication.

But packaging can also fog an argument. It can clutter and distract enough to cause us to miss some important aspect of the reasoning even when the speaker intends no deception. The most common embellishment of this sort is the use of jokes—a risky practice. If the joke fails, the embarrassment is usually acute. If it's funny, the humor can get in the way. We can all recall enjoying a speaker's jokes and later wondering by what logic he established his serious points.

Another kind of embellisher is the one who endlessly qualifies his claims:

> May I most cautiously venture to suggest the following: Certainly, and mainly because of the improbability of finding another job, you will, most likely—and provided you are adventurous enough—start your own business.

This example is hyperbole to the point of burlesque —an extravagant exaggeration for illustrative purposes. But even a line of reasoning with only half the boggle would be needlessly burdened. And how about this classic bit of fluff?

> POLONIUS (referring to Hamlet):
> My liege, and madam,—to expostulate
> What majesty should be, what duty is,
> Why day is day, night night, and time is time
> Were nothing but to waste night, day, and time.
> Therefore, since brevity is the soul of wit,
> And tediousness the limbs and outward flourishes,
> I will be brief:—your noble son is mad:
> Mad call I it; for, to define true madness,
> What is't but to be nothing else but mad?
> But let that go.
>
> QUEEN (by now sorely impatient):
> More matter with less art.
>
> *Hamlet* (II, ii)

✻   ✻   ✻

This about completes our first round with reasoning. We have, so far, sketched it very generally as a process of justifying or backing up a claim. By now, you may very well be asking a question I have not raised, except tangentially: the question of explanation. Yes, we reason when we give reasons for a claim, i.e., justify our believing in the truth of the claim. But don't we also reason when we give the causes at work behind an event—the causes which explain why the claim we're making is, in fact, true?

When we already know some claim to be true so that we need no further reasons for accepting it, we can still ask "Why is it true?" We know, for example, that the rate of breast cancer on Long Island is the highest in the country. We have plenty of evidence for this and are therefore already certain of it. But we'd sure like to know why. Note, we're still asking something about the truth of this claim. But now, instead of asking about the grounds on which to believe in the truth, we are asking about how it is to be explained.

In the next chapter, we will see how such an explanation is structured, and that it too is a genuine argument in which premises again end up serving as reasons in support of a conclusion.

4

CAUSES:
Explaining Our Surroundings

EXPLANATION: More Than Justification

The milk in my refrigerator smells like a garbage pail in August; it tastes lousy and looks curdled. On the basis of these reasons I am justified in concluding that the milk has gone sour. That is, the reasons are a *justification* for this conclusion. What they don't tell us, however, is why it went bad. That is, they don't explain the milk's being sour. To do this, I would have to know that there was an eight-hour power outage during which time the milk yielded to some milk-thirsty bacteria.

For another simple example, let's look in on Meg and Bert, who have just returned from a Caribbean cruise. Meg is making some telling observations about Bert's appearance:

Bert, You look a bit puffy this morning, and your belt is barely making it to the buckle. Also, your shirt collar is unbuttoned. Is it too tight? You've put on weight.

51

Her argument is a purely justificational one consisting of two premises and a conclusion. It can be paraphrased as follows:

1. Bert, you look puffy.
2. Your clothing seems a bit tight.
   Therefore
3. You have put on weight.

The two premises support or justify the conclusion; they give us reasons for believing in the truth of the final statement. But this argument does absolutely nothing to explain Bert's weight gain.

The needed explanation, however, comes soon enough when, only minutes later, Meg presses on with the following:

MEG: Sure, Bert, what did you do on that boat for ten days? You did what almost everyone does on Caribbean cruises. You ate nonstop.

To make matters worse, you don't dance and you hate shuffleboard. So when you weren't foraging at the bar or putting it away at the dining table, you were parked on the deck sipping colas and languidly converting calories into kilograms.

Little wonder you gained weight.

BERT: Yes, Meg, I know.

Without the strong overtones, Meg's reasoning amounts to the following:

Over the past three weeks, Bert, you have been drinking and
    eating excessively, and you have underexercised.
Therefore
You have gained weight.

Notice that the statements which Meg makes about Bert's activities are not primarily meant to justify the claim that Bert has gained weight. That justification has already been given in her first argument, and his weight gain has been essentially granted. The claim that Bert has gained weight therefore needs no further justification. What Meg intends to do in her second argument is something more; she wants to explain Bert's new poundage by saying what she thinks caused it.

THE JUSTIFICATION SIDE OF EXPLANATION

Explanations, however, also lend justification or support to their conclusions. I may, for example, point out that the children of my blue-eyed neighbors must also be blue-eyed because of the genetics involved. (Blue as an eye color is recessive. Therefore those with blue eyes are always genetically "pure" with respect to eye color, or else their eyes would not be blue. This means that two blue-eyed parents can never have non–blue-eyed children.) What we have here is of course an explanation, but, to some extent, it is also a justification for claiming (believing, asserting) that our neighbors' children do actually have blue eyes. In fact, if any doubt should arise regarding what we recall about the children's eye color, explaining why it must be blue would dispel that doubt.

More generally, then, knowing what caused some state of affairs does help convince us further of the actual existence of that state of affairs. This is why both finding a motive and reconstructing the events and circumstances leading to a crime are considered so crucial in establishing the guilt of any suspect. "Solving" a crime consists largely of discovering how and why the crime involved was committed, i.e., explaining it. Any prosecutor's case is weakened by a failure to provide such an explanation.

An example is the actual case of a Florida dentist and six of his patients: Epidemiologists from the federal Centers for Disease Control and Prevention cautiously concluded, on the basis of sophisticated DNA sequence tests, that the dentist had transmitted his HIV infection to the six patients. Despite the strong evidence (justification), controversy has recently flared up over this conclusion on arguable statistical grounds. The inconclusiveness in the case stems from the fact that no one has yet found an explanation of how the virus was actually transmitted from the dentist to the patients. Quoting one of the investigators: "The weakness of the case is that we don't know how transmission occurred."*

The justification side of explanation can be especially important in the case of a state of affairs that is not directly observable. For example, I may have some grounds for believing that when my television screen is on, it emits some (possibly harmful) invisible radiation. I may have concluded this on the basis some measurements with a detecting device like a geiger counter. But an explanation to the effect that, when the TV is on, very fast-moving electrons hit the oxide coating on the screen and produce X-rays would certainly strengthen my belief.

The additional support that explanations give is precisely what would prompt a remark like this:

> Ah-hah! Now that we know what Bert did for three weeks, we are not at all surprised by his weight gain. Had we known, we might have *expected* Bert to look as he does even before seeing him. Indeed, knowing how Bert spent his vacation assures us that there is nothing at all wrong with the scale he is using to weigh himself.

—or—

> Yes, Bob did smoke heavily all those years. The positive pathology "must" be correct. No point in repeating it.

Most interesting and important in all this is the case in which we know of the existence of the causes but have not yet observed the resulting events. This is nothing other than the case in which we predict the future or draw conclusions about the past. It is also the case when we draw conclusions about something happening right now but not accessible at the moment. In such cases, we are both explaining and justifying. Thus, knowing that Jones was heavily exposed to asbestos for thirty years not only ex-

---

*New York Times, July 5, 1994, p. C3.

plains Jones's having lung disease—if he actually does have it—
but it also constitutes strong grounds for believing that he has or
will soon have the disease, even when no actual symptoms have
yet appeared. For this reason, some physicians would urge frequent checkups for Jones. Similarly, women whose ancestors
have had breast cancer would probably be advised to be especially alert in this regard even though there are no present clinical signs of disease.

EXPLANATIONS AS REAL ARGUMENTS

There is a tendency with some authors of logic texts to disregard
explanation as a form of reasoning—a tendency that seems
strange to begin with. What could possibly be more like reasoning than explaining something? This tendency may be due to
the mistaken idea that explanations do nothing other than cite
causes. If so, they are not arguments simply because arguments
—in order to be arguments—must consist of a conclusion and a
set of premises which support or justify that conclusion.

The account we have already given of the justificational
nuance in any explanation hints strongly against this view. But to
this we can add a more conclusive consideration. The very concept of explanation involves more than merely mentioning
causes. True, when we explain a fire we ordinarily mention only
the faulty electric wiring, or the smoking in bed, or the defective
space heater, or the lighting. We do this only for brevity. The
events or circumstances that we mention are causes only in the
sense that they are related to their effects in terms of some natural law, pattern, or regularity. A more explicit explanation of
Bert's weight gain would therefore include mention of such a
law and take the form of an argument like the following:

(Causal law) People who eat a lot and exercise little usually
gain weight.

(Cause) Bert did just that for three weeks.
Therefore (Probably)
(Effect) Bert gained weight during the cruise.

The first premise is a rough, statistical law of nature that connects heavy eating and little exercising with weight gain. The second premise cites the actual causes—namely the activities which led to Bert's weight gain. Finally, the conclusion mentions the resulting effect of these activities on Bert. The two premises together, if true, give support to the conclusion by making it probable. They therefore not only explain the conclusion, but, if true, also constitute grounds for believing it.

Summarizing, we see that reasoning employs two sorts of arguments. Some arguments simply justify a conclusion without explaining it, as when I cite a scale reading to support concluding that I've gained weight. Other arguments go further and also explain, as when we cite Bert's conduct (the relevant law being understood), as a cause of his weight gain.

* * *

Our account so far has been about reasoned discourse or arguments. In attempting to communicate, however, we sometimes either talk through both sides of our mouths or talk empty altogether. In the next chapter, we'll see how we sometimes lapse into these "blank" modes of discourse.

5

NONSENSE:
Viruses in Our Knowledge;
Emptiness in Our Talk

INCONSISTENCY

When were you last either *be*-mused or *a*-mused by an inconsistent statement? I recently had both feelings after leaving a wedding one evening when, as it happened, I asked one of my companions (who may have had too much merlot) if he had a tip for the valet who had parked our car.

He replied, "Sorry, my smallest is a five from the change I got a moment ago when I collected our coats." So I asked, "Oh yes, what did that coat check cost—so we can square up?"

"Let me see. It cost four dollars. I gave her a twenty and got back sixteen."

A more befuddling remark is one attributed to George Bernard Shaw: "Experience teaches that men learn absolutely nothing from experience."

The shaky logical integrity in these examples is more or less obvious. In each of them there is an inconsistency. This simply means that in each of them, the authors make some particular claim which, in effect, they then go on to withdraw.

The crudest and most obvious way of being inconsistent is to commit a flat or patent contradiction. This is done by making some statement and then immediately or flatly denying that very same statement:

- The beer is cold; yet it's not cold.
- My house is not my house!
- Even as I told nothing but the truth, I lied unscrupulously.

Sentences like these are about as jarring to our linguistic sense as musical discords are to our tonal sense. Taken literally, they are flat or patent contradictions. Their inconsistency is obvious, and we therefore rarely "contradict ourselves" in this manner. When we do, usually someone quickly corrects us.

IMPLICIT INCONSISTENCIES

The subtle way of being inconsistent is to do it implicitly. This sort of inconsistency is, of course, harder to detect and therefore more common. Our Bernard Shaw example is an implicit inconsistency. It does not explicitly contain a claim and its denial, but, at least on one interpretation, it implies such a thing. Take Shaw's comment to be an argument whose conclusion is that we learn nothing from experience. The reason he offers is that experience teaches something, which in this context, we can take to mean that we learn something from experience. Shaw's remark, therefore, comes down to:

> We learn something from experience.
> and
> We learn nothing from experience.

And this of course is a patent contradiction.

Here are other implicit inconsistencies—again, for simplicity, rather obvious ones:

- I absolutely never eat anything before retiring but when I'm out late, I get back so famished that before flopping into bed, I pig out on anything I can get my hands on.
- The bachelor next door is married.
- Mom, please cut that tart in the middle, and give me the larger half.
- I have no problem with that group; I just don't approve of their lifestyle.

And, that old one:

- What happens when an irresistible force runs up against an immovable object?

As ordinarily understood, this last question presupposes that an irresistible force and an immovable object can both exist. That such a claim couches a contradiction is easily seen once we realize that the idea of an irresistible force is incompatible with that of an object that can resist any force. The implied contradiction can be expressed as follows:

There exists a force, F, and an object, O, such that F can move any object, and O cannot be moved by any force.

And this of course is tantamount to saying that:

There is a force, F, and an object, O, such that F can move O and F cannot move O.

The absurdity in contradictions sometimes elevates them to the level of gags:

- I'm not afraid to die; I just don't want to be there when it happens.
- I'd give my right arm to be ambidextrous.
- Yes, I know that everything is exactly what it is. Yet things are more like they used to be than like they are now.

A note on the kitchen table from a peevish seven-year-old:

> I hate you, Mommy.
> Love, Peter

CONTEXTUAL INCONSISTENCIES

Some statements "smack" of inconsistency not because they, by themselves, harbor contradictions, but because of the shared background of knowledge against which they are made. The statement in question is usually an argument and the background knowledge context becomes a set of implicit assumptions about the subject matter involved. Our very first example about money and change is a contextual inconsistency.

My companion's claim of having nothing less than a five plus what we all know about the denominations of paper money tell us that he had to have either at least one single or some two-dollar bills. But this, together with his reply implies (implicitly contains) the patent contradiction:

> I have nothing less than a five and I have something less than a five.

Contextual inconsistencies are the kind of inconsistencies we most often commit because the contradictions they harbor can be especially elusive:

> To balance our budgets and reduce public debt, we had better cut down on government assistance programs. This means not

only putting more welfare recipients to work, but also cutting job training programs along with child care facilities and other handouts that tend to institutionalize indolence and dependency.

The author of this speech is recommending "workfare" over welfare but forgetting that putting people to work is facilitated by job training and child care centers.

I say, thumbs down on capital punishment. To begin with, it is far less punishing and therefore less feared than loss of liberty for the rest of one's life without the possibility of parole. This means that of the two, capital punishment is the less effective deterrent. Secondly, capital punishment discriminates adversely against the poor, since, as we all know, a poor defendant is more likely to be death-sentenced than a wealthy one.

The author of this argument cannot seem to make up his mind as to which alternative is more punishing.

CONTRADICTIONS ARE NOT JUST FALSE

Contradictions obviously lie at the heart of inconsistency, so, let's take a closer look at them. Exactly what is wrong with them? How do they instantly muddle communication? Why are they so confusing, embarrassing, and as entrapping as barbed-wire cages once we're caught in them?

In the first place, they're at least false. The person next door cannot be a bachelor and also married. Anyone who understands the words "bachelor" and "married" knows this. Secondly, the falsity of contradictions differs in an enormously important way from the falsity of "ordinary" or garden variety falsehoods.

- The moon is made of cheese.
- Men have one rib less than women.
- The number of solar planets is eight.

These three statements are ordinary falsehoods. They are matter-of-fact statements whose falsehood we establish by examining the actual objects involved: the moon, the human anatomy, the solar system. We do this by observing these objects with our senses or reading what others have observed about them.

These same sentences, though, could conceivably have been true. They would be true in a different kind of world—that is, one in which the moon *was* made of cheese, the number of solar planets *was* eight, and men *did* generally have one rib less than women. For this reason, such falsehoods are more technically known as *contingent falsehoods,* meaning by this that their falsity is contingent (depends) on what the world (the moon, the planets, men, women, etc.) happens to be like.

The falsity of a contradiction, however, is of a very different sort and has absolutely nothing to do with what the world is actually like. It depends only on linguistic form, and this form is

S and not-S

where S is any statement at all and not-S is the denial of that very same statement.

Any statement having this form cannot possibly be true. It simply *must* be false. To see this, consider any statement consisting of two smaller statements that are connected by the word "and." Now, if we know the truth of the smaller statements, what can we say about the combination? The answer is that we regard such a compound statement, considered in its entirety, as true when and only when both its parts are true. For example, we would regard the whole statement "Paris is the capital of France, and Paris is south of the equator," as false because its second component is in fact false.

We can now see how any statement having a contradictory form must be false, no matter what. Obviously, negation reverses the truth-value of any statement. This means that the two "sides" of a contradiction must have opposite truth-values. A contradiction, therefore, will always have one false side, thereby making it (the composite statement) always false—no matter what happens anywhere else, anytime. Whereas plain falsehoods are *contingently* false, contradictions are false for all possible circumstances or, more dramatically, for all possible worlds. Philosophers like to put this by saying that they are *necessarily* false.

A LETHAL WEAPON

This arms us with a lethal but user-friendly weapon. The lethal part is that we can refute any statement by showing either that it is a contradiction or that it implies one. The user-friendly part is that to do this, we need only study the statement itself so as to make out its form or analyze it further for what it implies. We need engage in no other kind of investigation. The process is, as we might say, a purely "logical" one in which matters of fact do not figure at all. This means we don't have to look in Fred's pockets, or inquire about how people learn, or otherwise expand our information beyond what we already have.

From the viewpoint of critical thinking, this is a profoundly important result. Just think of it. As long as we understand the language of any claim, we can challenge its consistency, and, when we have uncovered a contradiction in that claim, we have falsified it decisively. Most remarkable, if not simply astounding, is the fact that, paradoxically enough, we can do all this even when we know less about the subject than the very author of the claim.

USED CAR OWNER: My price is absolutely firm. I am the original owner of this solid little car which has taken me faithfully to and from work every workday of every year since I bought it five years ago. It has a total of 95,000 miles on it and a factory rebuilt clutch which I put in only a few months ago.

CUSTOMER: I have never driven a standard shift. How many miles can you get on a clutch?

USED CAR OWNER: Oh, these Honda clutches do okay. I got 55,000 miles on my original one even though I was first learning five-speed and was very hard on it.

CUSTOMER: And how many miles per year have you been putting on the car?

USED CAR OWNER: Almost exactly 19,000 miles every year since the beginning.
    Would you like to drive it?

CUSTOMER: I don't know beans about cars, so driving it will tell me nothing. But you, sir, seem to be talking through both sides of your mouth. You claim your new clutch went in only a few months ago. Yet you say you got 55,000 miles out of the original one, which means that you replaced it more like two years ago and have already heaped 40,000 miles on the second one. As a rebuilt, it may already be going. And, your price, on which you won't budge, does not reflect any of this.
    Goodbye, I'm going elsewhere for a new car.

Looking for inconsistency is one of the most basic and powerful strategies of discourse. The search, which should be relentless, is the very signature of the critical thinker. It may be trivially easy or monumentally difficult depending the subtleties involved. But, the power of a positive finding is devastating.

THE ULTIMATE KNOCK-DOWN METHOD:
Cross-Examination

In situations where the reasoners are adversaries or even just competitors, as, for example, in courtrooms, boardrooms, or political forums, catching an opponent in contradiction is the ultimate knock-down strategy which will almost always crush even the most authoritative interlocutor. Attorneys know this and in cross-examining their unfavorable witnesses they sometimes push them into contradiction. The payoff is that, as we have already seen, when this happens it becomes absolutely certain that some portion of what the witness is saying is, as a matter of fact, plainly false.

A cross-examination by a defense attorney might go something like this:

> Is this the man that you saw half a block away as you stepped out of your car in New York this past December, at about 6:00 P.M.?
> Yes, it is.
> Would you have been able to make him out from that distance if it had been night time?
> No, but there was still some daylight in which to see him clearly as I stepped out of my car.
> Well then, did you notice the large writing in yellow chalk on your front door, as you opened it to enter at just about that time?
> Yes.
> And did you try to read it?
> Yes, I did.
> Can you tell us what that writing said?
> No, it was already too dark for me to quite make it out.

The index of suspicion for inconsistency seems high in this witness's testimony. His answers add up to the patent contradiction:

> There was enough light for clear visibility, and there was not enough light for clear visibility.

VIRUSES IN OUR KNOWLEDGE

In passing we might just mention here a related but crucial theoretical objection to contradictions. In science and mathematics a theory is typically a set of general assumptions. The on-going hope in these disciplines is that any theory with whose help conclusions are being drawn is consistent or free of contradiction.

The abstractness of some theories and the subtleties of their concepts can make it difficult to decide anything about their consistencies. Because of this, a theory may be in full use long before its consistency has been satisfactorily demonstrated. In fact, the consistency of some theories often remains an open question for a long time, even for centuries. This has happened over and over again throughout the history of science and mathematics.

Remarkably enough, however, even from inconsistent theories we can draw true conclusions. This becomes apparent once we realize that in an inconsistent theory there may be other implicit content besides a contradiction—some of it possibly true. We may recall also that the contradictory content itself, like all contradictions, has two sides, not only a false component but also a true one.

The big trouble, however, is that if there is a contradiction in a theory, that theory must—as we have seen—harbor some falsehood which, like a hidden virus, can pop out unexpectedly when we reason on the basis of that theory. This is why theorists expend large amounts of effort searching for and detecting hidden inconsistencies in theories. When these are found, the theories can be scrubbed "clean" to fend off the possibility of their leading to false conclusions.

THE OXYMORON

Now, a word of caution. You have no doubt encountered statements that appear to be inconsistent but on careful reflection turn out to make some sense—sometimes with considerable poignancy. Statements of this sort, known as oxymorons, can be very effective in figurative and poetic expression. Here are some examples from the German philosopher Nietzsche, who was a master of this device. These are taken from his most famous book, *Thus Spoke Zarathustra*:

"Thus Spoke Zarathustra: A Book for All and None."

"They are jubilant if for once you are modest enough to be vain."

"What does he know of love who did not despise precisely what he loved?"

"God is dead."

"I love the great despisers because they are the great reverers."

Here are some examples from more ordinary contexts:

He killed me with kindness.

She was eloquent with her silence.

Some humans are simply not human.

Some people believe in telling *all* the truths, even those that are not true.

I'm not working hard at all these days and I'm working hard at keeping it that way.

Vision is the ability to see things that are invisible. (Jonathan Swift)

HARRY: You should do all your smoking, Bert, when no one is around. The smoke is very annoying and possibly harmful.

BERT: Yes I know, Harry. It's a very bad habit. I should do all my smoking when even *I'm* not around.

The flavor of inconsistency in the statement about some humans not being human calls attention to the difference between being biologically human and possessing the personal qualities that not all humans have but perhaps should have. Similarly, Nietzsche's claim that God is dead could be taken to mean not that some immortal being has done what only mortals can do (a contradiction), but that the concept 'god' is no longer operative in human affairs, or perhaps even that it is no longer acceptable.

The rhetorical kick in oxymorons lies in what at first blush appears to be blatant inconsistency. This gives them shock value together with a measure of obscurity that lends an aura of profundity to what is being said. Still, the artful use of this figurative device can add real interest and texture to a passage. It is, therefore, generally rewarding to interpret oxymorons charitably by making the effort to see in them the possible shifts of meaning that rescue them from contradiction. Interpretations of this sort, of course, depend heavily on context and must be made carefully.

We might want to say, however, that those texts which use such locutions in too breezy a manner can seriously fog meaning and be rightly judged profoundly obscure rather than obscurely profound.

EMPTY TALK: Tautology

You have no doubt read or heard statements that left you blank or saying, "Did I miss something?" The problem this time was not inconsistency. The statement was true and, of course, perfectly consistent, but there was something needlessly repetitious or trivially obvious about it. Worse still, it was somehow empty of content, leaving you not one bit more informed or enlightened about the subject than you were before.

Whenever this has happened chances are you encountered a tautology, perhaps not an obvious one, but one nonetheless.

Here are some tautologies—most of them so obvious as to seem silly or trivial:

Either Shakespeare died in 1616 or he did not die in 1616.

If the Dodgers stay ahead of the Mets until the very end of the game, they will most surely win.

We are all mortal, and so we must die.

All bachelors are unmarried.

Every pentagon has five sides.

In ordinary discourse, you would not take any of these statements very seriously, probably considering them repetitious and tedious, some of them being more objectionable in this respect than others. But there is one thing we can say for all of them: They are certainly true, though trivially so.

The trouble is that the truth of tautologies reflects only the meanings of the words with which they are expressed or, more generally, the rules of the language in which they are imbedded. For this reason, they are, as we sometimes say, "true by definition." That is, they're merely verbal truths that follow necessarily from the meanings involved. Because of this, the truth of tautologies is entirely independent of anything else in the world; they communicate no factual information at all about their subject matter. Their truth is determined not by material fact, but by linguistic conventions generally understood and followed by all those who correctly use the language involved. Therefore, once we accept the rules of the language in which tautologies are uttered, we must accept them as true. They are as *necessarily true* as contradictions are necessarily false, and just as factually empty. Little wonder, then, that statements of this sort (though necessarily true) leave us so entirely blank!

To help fix our ideas, let's pause for a closer look at some of our examples.

The truth of our first example (about Shakespeare's death), follows necessarily from the very concept of statement together with what we mean by the words "not" and "or." To see this, all we have to do is agree that part of what we mean by saying that something is a statement is that, by definition, it is something which is either true or false. The statement, "Shakespeare died in 1616," therefore, must be either true or false, no matter what is or is not true of anything else. This is equivalent to saying that, necessarily, "Either Shakespeare died in 1616 or Shakespeare did not die in 1616." This last statement therefore is true, not on the basis of any particular fact about Shakespeare, but only by virtue of the rules of the very language in which the statement is expressed. For that matter, it is also (necessarily) true that either

Shakespeare died in 1997 or Shakespeare did not die in 1997. Moreover, any statement of this form would be true not only of Shakespeare but of any other mortal we might wish to mention.

Our second example: Shakespeare is identical with Shakespeare (i.e., Shakespeare = Shakespeare) also follows merely from what we mean by the concept of identity and the concept of object, Shakespeare being the object. Any statement of this form would be true of any object we care to mention. The statements in the remaining examples are also similarly seen to be true by virtue of what we mean by the words in them, e.g., "end of the game," "win," "mortal," "die," "bachelor," "unmarried," "pentagon," "five sides," and so on, rather than because of any particular state of affairs anywhere in the world. Part of what the term "bachelor" means is "unmarried," and part of what the term "pentagon" means is "having five sides." "All bachelors are unmarried" and "All pentagons have five sides" are therefore nothing but empty truisms based on no more than a reiteration of meaning. The same can be said of the last two examples. Recall how our composition teachers damned such statements as a tautologies? When they did this, they were objecting to their uninformative, repetitious content.

The parallelism and antiparallelism between tautologies and contradictions is rather obvious, yet fascinating. Though contradictions are false and tautologies are true, they are these things necessarily and therefore, independently of any matter of fact. This means we can extract from them no information at all about ships, sealing wax, or anything else.

We might also note that just as inconsistencies are not all transparent contradictions, tautologies are not all one-liner truisms. Some—although only little—reflection is needed to see all the redundancies in the following statement:

> The right of every law-abiding citizen to bear defensive firearms is the right of anyone who has never violated the law and who, as a certified member of our society, ought not be prevented from carrying a gun for self-defense.

Tautologous content is sometimes funny:

Why is it that we always find what we're looking for in the very last place we look?

Having children is hereditary. If your parents didn't have any, you won't either.

SEEMING TAUTOLOGIES THAT ARE NOT REALLY TAUTOLOGIES

Just as there are statements called oxymorons which look inconsistent but really aren't, there are statements which look tautologous but really aren't. Here, for example, is one: "Too much caution is not good."

Only a pedant or a sophist would take this sentence literally. Its predicate seems to repeat what is already contained in the subject term, "too much caution," for if anything is too much it is of course not good. Read more charitably, however, the sentence tells us that one can be too cautious; this, of course, is by no means a tautology.

Pain is pain.

Survival is survival.

Love is love.

You gotta do what you gotta do.

These statements have the form of patent tautologies, but in the appropriate contexts, they are really saying something:

Pain is absolutely distasteful.

Survival is a must.

Love is irrepressible.

There are times when your conscience compels you to act.

Interpreted in these ways, the original sentences are neither empty, needlessly repetitious, nor trivial. Rather than being tautologous they are dramatic ways of casting and communicating some of our general but factually significant observations.

Incidentally, it occurs to me that, though we have the term "oxymoron" for apparent contradictions that are not really so, no one has yet coined a name for apparent tautologies that are not really tautologies. Wouldn't it be nice to have one, given that such locutions can be so effective in figurative communication? How about "oxytauton"? Too big a mouthful, I suppose.

*   *   *

Having gone this far into our subject let us pause for two haunting questions: How adversarial and how charitable should the critical thinker be? Can reasoning tyrannize us and spoil all the fun? On to our next chapter for possible answers.

6

HAUNTING ISSUES:
Charity and Tyranny

CHARITY: Dancing with the Other—
A Win-Win Move

Virtually all societies regard generosity as a high moral virtue. Should we honor this principle in critical thinking? The answer here must be yes. In reasoned discourse, charity is more than virtue; it is smart. It is the response most likely to face the main thrust of any argument squarely and deal with it effectively.

Imagine someone, for example, offering the following argument:

> It is time we react intelligently to the amount of violence in our movies and television programs. Enough public concern expressed in our newspapers and elsewhere can inspire some high level studies on the short- and long-term effects of continued exposure to this kind of entertainment. If it turns out that there is good reason for believing it to be socially and psy-

chologically damaging, strong appeals can be made to the industry for some self-regulation. Our psyches as well as our society are vulnerable, and the stakes are therefore high.

This would be an uncharitable and misplaced objection:

> There is at present no cause whatever for panic. First of all, not all violence need worry us, especially when our entertainment serves justice by having the bad guys get what they deserve. Furthermore, what we know about the psychological and societal effects of audio-visual material is fraught with such uncertainty that we need better knowledge of "what can cause what" before we sound the alarm and make sweeping recommendations. If violence in present-day society is the problem, then let us look at the underlying social problems like poverty, job opportunities, and education.

The objection misses the point of the original argument, which is that there is enough violence in the media to warrant thought about its short- and long-term effects. Serious studies are in order, and if these show damaging effects, we should make strong appeals to the industry for some self-regulation.

Interpreted charitably, this argument, though showing concern, is hardly to be characterized as a cry of panic. It makes no claim about our state of knowledge on the issue. The recommendations are constructive and modest rather than sweeping. They call for discussion, research, and, depending on the findings, a rational appeal to the industry. Most certainly, the argument nowhere excludes concerning ourselves with other societal issues like poverty and education.

We could of course go overboard and play games with contentious sophisms. What about the endless number of unstated assumptions that the arguer obviously takes for granted? How does she know that somewhere down the road there will not be a global catastrophe to annihilate us all before entertainment violence does? Are short-lived profits *really* less valuable than more durable, deferred ones? Mightn't our lives be more interesting with the challenge and excitement of widespread violence? What about extinction in a sea of violence? Would it *really* be the worst thing for an unhappy world like ours? Needless to say, raising objections like these where serious reasoning is going on is just disruptive mischief.

One of the most common but uncharitable retorts to almost any argument is the "not necessarily" one. How many times have you heard it or said it yourself? I, myself, have still not succeeded in completely shedding this vacuous and irritating mannerism:

SALESMAN: Our reduced sales last year could very well have been due to the mild winter.

SALES MANAGER: (uncharitably): Not necessarily so. It could simply have been a random shift in consumer preference.

SALESMAN: (charitably): I know what you mean, but I think it was, more likely, the weather.

The charitable and more plausible interpretation of the salesman's remark is that he is offering only a probable opinion rather than a certainty. Fortunately, he, himself, manages to avoid an uncharitable response like, "I didn't say, *necessarily.*"

There is much justification for being charitable in reasoning. Uncharitable interpretations have little constructive value. Instead of moving the reasoning along, they frustrate and disrupt it by focusing on whatever is vulnerable. Critical thinking is not verbal skirmishing in order to win by hook or crook. It is reasoning, not debating. The goal is not to get the better of the other reasoner, but to sift out, understand, and appraise what she intended, even when she has not expressed herself as clearly or as convincingly as she might have.

More importantly, the uncharitable responses are the more risky ones. In serious reasoning there is likely to be enough solid content to make reading for the best possible sense the far more realistic approach, the one more likely to capture whatever the reasoner intended. Nettling weak spots, raising trivial objections, and distorting an opposed argument in order to knock it down are all gimmicky distractions—fruitless errors of missing the main point that are just waiting to happen.

DANCING WITH THE ENEMY

The recommendation to be charitable remains in full force even with an adversary, and for good reason. To do otherwise is like failing to take cognizance of his full range of fire. We should always try to get a hold on the thrust of our opponent's argument. Without such a hold, how can we respond effectively? In addition, responding constructively can help sustain full communication and thus heighten the chances of interactive enlightenment and reasoned accord. This being the case, dancing with the enemy promises much more than exchanging fire with him. It is, as some would put it, the "logical way to go."

The principle of charity, of course, always entails the risk of reading too much into an argument. Surely some arguments are so bad that they should be either corrected or scotched altogether. Failure to be charitable, however, seems still to be the riskier side on which to err.

WHY REASON? Tyranny or Freedom?

A gnawing question arises here. The practical imperative which bids us to reason is a compelling one. We sense that if we don't reason, we risk serious and regrettable error. Also, recall in this connection what we called the "logical force" of reasons. A good argument, once we listen to it, is a powerful, even if resistible, force. Our question, then, is this: What does this force do to us? Does reasoning coerce and subject us to the point of diminishing our freedom to choose according to our true desires? Does it inhibit us from doing and thinking what we really want to do and think?

It is Saturday morning, and I feel a sweeping urge to get back to the races where I lost nearly a week's salary last night and resolved never to come back. But this morning I have that "racy" feeling which tells me that today can be the start of a winning streak. I can recoup some of my past losses and maybe even get a little ahead of the game. That would be the time to quit. But darn it—I have a paddle-ball appointment with Jack.

Paddle-ball? Great aerobic exercise! But how dull compared to the thunderous excitement of the race! I'll call him and say I'm not quite up to it today. He won't come to the race-track—says gambling is expensive and disruptive. And he's so right—as he's always been on this whole issue.

Good heavens, I *am* addicted—addicted to a consuming, insatiable passion! But, surely I can still kick it in time to reconstitute my crumbling existence and even save my marriage. If I go back today, I will have succumbed once more, and when the excitement is over, I'll lose, no matter how I do on the betting. Indeed, doing well today will only feed my enthusiasm for doing it again, and doing badly will only make recouping my losses more urgent. Either way I'll be at it again tomorrow and the next day and so on. It could all even spell suicide by the end of the year. No, the track is madness. No track today; no track tomorrow; no track ever! Where are the paddles?

The reasoning in this case is certainly persuasive, and it seems to be prevailing over impulse. But now ask: Is there some insidious tyranny at work here, some "tyranny of reason" which can usurp our freedom and block off free choice in very much the same way blind sweeping forces sometimes do? Does reasoning tend to throw a wet blanket on the fun in us? Who is the one that ultimately gathers more rosebuds, the thinker or the swinger?

Calling reasoning a tyrant is a familiar personification that echoes a reaction to the sort of rationalism, traceable to Plato, that narrowly subordinates feelings to rationality. Catchy as it sounds, though, this metaphor seriously oversimplifies the role of reasoning in human action.

Reasoning, unlike impulse, does not compel us by limiting or obscuring our options. Instead it throws light on their full range, and it does this by bringing out the likely consequences of any option. How else can we gauge the burning urgency of an immediate want against the pale promise of a long-term objective or of some abstract moral principle? Rather than forcing our choices, reasoning sponsors them. It is our first step toward choosing rationally. By "rationally" we mean "consistently, with priorities that are ordered in accordance with how deeply and consistently we value them." By widening our vision in this way, reasoning empowers us to choose what we really want as opposed to what we think we want at the moment. What we have here is not imposition but informed choice, not subjection but self-culturing and self-regulation. No person is more autonomous than one who reasons and is free to live by her conclusions. If this is so, then reasoning must rank high, not as tyrant, but as something vital to *real* personal freedom and ultimately to a free and open society.

Nor does it matter who the author of any line of reasoning is as long as the reasoning is good. Had the reasoning in my dilemma come from my paddle-ball partner instead of me, the result would have been the same, providing that I had grasped his argument and judged it a good one. As soon as I have understood and approved an argument, no matter who first offered it, I have, *ipso facto,* made it entirely my own. If I act on it, I act with no less conviction than if I had been the one to offer it in the first place. No one, therefore, tyrannizes me by persuading me with acceptable arguments. I accept them because I comprehend them and find them convincing. When I have responded in this way, I have suffered no indignity. Nor have I surrendered any sovereignty to any other will.

Okay, let us grant that the power of reasoning is persuasion and not coercion. Isn't it still the case, however, that in its ultimate overall effect reasoning inevitably undermines or even smothers many of the passions that give zest to life and keep me going? And if so, wouldn't a strong commitment to reasoning tend to stifle the most spirited and joyous part of me and lead me into the dank dungeons of asceticism?

The answer to this is nearly as old as philosophy itself. Reasoning, as many thinkers have recognized, is not in any basic sense opposed to or incompatible with emotional fulfillment. On the contrary, and unlike impulse, it helps define and prioritize our needs so as to maximize, not stifle, their timely satisfaction. Is there any better way of hedging our decisions against crippling error? A poetic line from Shakespeare's *King Richard II* about our needs may be worth quoting here: "Teach thy necessity to reason . . ." (I, iii).

Or, in John Dewey's words, "Reasoning governs not as a tyrant from without, but as a guide to which impulses and emotions are gladly responsive" ("Virtues," from *Ethics*).

＊　＊　＊

This first part of our book has been about reasoning in general with a view toward outlining its broadest features. Becoming explicitly familiar with these features is, I believe, a first move toward establishing some of the self-monitoring, critical orientation we can all use.

Our discussion so far also yields a few practical guidelines which we can cull together and summarize for instant application in virtually any context. Let's give these the form of a protocol consisting of "key" questions. Faced with an argument in an editorial, at a board meeting, in a political speech, or even in ordinary conversation, asking some "right questions" can help immensely in deciding quickly whether to accept, reject, or hold off.

Our next chapter is a mini-manual which itemizes nine such questions.

7

ASKING THE RIGHT QUESTIONS:
A Mini-Manual for the Critical Thinker

The following set of nine "right questions" will come in handy in responding to the claims and arguments that incessantly confront us in our everyday activities. They will also highlight some key points made in our discussion so far.

1. *Is there any inconsistency in the account?* Or, to put it differently, is what is being said free of contradiction?

This is the rock-bottom question in all communication. As we've already noted in some detail, inconsistency not only muddles things, it also blots out truth. Charged with a clearly demonstrated contradiction, any claim is almost fatally wounded requiring the most intensive emergency medicine if some version or remnant of it is to be salvaged. What is more, except for very technical contexts, contradictions—even implied ones—are not hard to spot if we give some careful attention to the concepts and claims being presented. Checking for consistency, therefore, can pay handsome discussion dividends.

More charitably, however, in detecting inconsistencies, we

aim primarily not to torpedo arguments but to deliver them from the crunch of contradiction. Expunging inconsistency from a text is a major step toward moving the thinking further along.

2. *What argument does the account offer?* What is the conclusion—usually the main point—and what reasons are given in support of it?

Remember those reading comprehension questions calling for "main points" on standardized aptitude tests, company exams, law boards, etc.? Isolating the bare-bones argument is the surest way to cut through such thickets. It almost always isolates the main point of any reasoned text.

In this strategy, it is important to avoid a very common error, namely that of confusing the author's conclusion with her purposes or agenda. Conclusions are claims (statements, propositions) which the author arrives at by reasoning. Purposes, on the other hand, are not part of the reasoning. In fact, they're not claims at all. They are intentions that reflect what the author wishes to achieve by reasoning to her conclusion. They motivate (cause) the reasoning, but do not constitute it.

3. *Are the reasons which the author gives in support of her conclusion acceptable?* If the truth of any reason is doubtful, can it be supported by still other reasons? Clearly, to the extent that any premise (reason, assumption) remains seriously doubtful, it fails to support the conclusion and must therefore be either further justified or else dropped from the argument.

4. *How relevant are the reasons?* Even if the premises are true, how well do they connect logically with the conclusion? If they don't, they're irrelevant and do not make an argument.

The important question, then, is, how do we gauge the amount of support even true premises give a conclusion? How strong is the resulting argument?

This question strikes at the heart of all reasoning. We will not attempt to answer it at this point in our discussion, continuing, instead, to rely, for the time being, on our natural abilities for making judgments of relevance. Part three, where we take a much closer look at both deductive and indeductive reasoning, will be devoted to answering this most basic question of logic.

5. *Are there any questionable, hidden (unstated, implicit) assumptions which the author makes in support of his conclusion?* Keep in mind here that only those implicit assumptions which are questionable need be considered.

It is also immensely helpful to determine whether these are factual or value assumptions. Keep in mind that value assumptions reflect either moral or aesthetic orientations and are therefore the ones more likely to pose huge roadblocks.

6. *Are there doubts about the meaning of any word or phrase in the argument?* Obviously without semantic agreement, we are not both having the same conversation.

7. *Are there widely held reasons against the conclusion?* An old saying has it that "anyone who does not know the arguments on the other side knows very little about his subject."

There is hardly an issue worth thinking about that is so simple that any position on it will not be subject to some serious objections. In arguing most effectively we often do well not only to present all our reasons *for* a position, but also to address the known reasons *against* it. Recognizing and addressing negative reasons or objections even before they are levelled against us by an opponent obviously requires a full acquaintance with the various facets of the issue. Negative reasons must be shown to be either false or else irrelevant to the matter at hand. Otherwise they must be given their due weight in the "net" or overall justification of the position we are defending.

At any rate, if the aim of reasoning is to present reasonable arguments and hence arrive at the most plausible conclusions, relevant negative reasons should not be swept under—even if a full recognition of them means reversing our own position. On the other hand, an essay in which the author anticipates and successfully answers possible objections will be far more convincing than one that does not. Indeed, it can pull the rug out from under the very feet of the opposition.

Handbooks on how to win debates of course will caution

against helping your opponents by anticipating objections they might never have thought of on their own. But, as we have already noted, well-reasoned argumentation is not debating. Its objective is not to prevail but to arrive at the best answers. What we might call pro–con balance in reasoned presentations about complex issues is one of the most distinguishing marks of the more highly sophisticated reasoner in any subject.

8. *Tautology?* Tautologies, though tedious and empty, are not in themselves grave logical offenses. They are neither false nor detracting from the soundness or validity of any piece of reasoning. Still, they should be quickly recognized for what they are: repetitious, trivial truisms that, if not politely disposed of, can be distracting and time-consuming. There is virtually nothing more annoying, even in the most friendly discourse, than someone seriously making such pronouncements as "We all ought to do what is right," or "Americans prefer baseball to soccer because baseball is their favorite national sport." When delivered with oratorical flourish and a few embellishments, such prattle can, even if only for a moment, usurp our energies and attention as we strain to see some content.

9. *How charitably are we reading the text?* We have already outlined several reasons for being charitable in critical discourse. Most of all, charity is the better bet for keeping the cross-hairs of argument on the major points for a better shot at enlightened agreement.

✳   ✳   ✳

Our armamentarium for critical thinking is still far from complete. It will be expanded and considerably strengthened in the next part of this book where we will discuss ways of deceiving ourselves and others known as *standard fallacies*. Though the fallacies we'll discuss are elusive, we can easily familiarize ourselves with them in order to avoid them. The next part of our discussion is a close-up of these dangerous and deceptive but avoidable pitfalls.

Part Two

FALLACIES:
Seduction and Deception

8

THE MOST DECEPTIVE TWISTS OF LOGIC:
Know Them to Avoid Them

Logic and rhetoric make men able to contend.

Francis Bacon
The Advancement of Learning (1605)

A SPECIAL KIND OF BAD REASONING

Do you know anyone who does not, from time to time, make mistakes in reasoning—even serious ones? Just go to seminars of physicists, mathematicians, computer scientists, literary critics, diagnosticians, philosophers, logicians, or any others who are generally supposed to be expert reasoners and watch the more discursive contributions and exchanges—possibly during the question-and-answer periods. Watch the uncertainty, stumblings, disagreements, and backtracking in their reasoning. It doesn't seem to matter how advanced the group. Try even a meeting of Nobel laureates.

Reasoning is a subtle activity in which slip-ups and oversights can always occur as we move from a set of premises to a conclusion. Even experts, reasoning closely and carefully in their special areas, make mistakes. The history of mathematics is a graveyard of reasoned "proofs" once thought perfect and later found defective. In the natural sciences practitioners are forever correcting and amending the misjudgments and misconceptions of their predecessors. Fortunately, these errors are usually no more than incidental blunders which we eventually recognize and correct or just let pass as testimony to our human fallibility.

Over the centuries, however, logicians have carefully singled out various modes of defective reasoning which have come to be known as fallacies. Here is an example of one type from an old television comedy:

EDITH: Archie, do you think God really exists?

ARCHIE: Of course, Dingbat. It says so in the Bible, and the Bible is the word of God.

Archie's reasoning is not only wrong, it is misleading, evasive, and circular. With enough such responses, one can muddle or even stonewall any discussion.

Fallacies are more than just mistakes. They're types of arguments that seem correct but actually aren't. This makes them elusive and beguiling enough to be dangerously seductive, especially when we are emotionally susceptible and are being told the things we want to hear.

A QUICK REMEDY FOR AN OLD AFFLICTION

Fallacious arguments are so convincing that they are committed (and have probably always been committed) with a frequency and range nothing short of pandemic. It is no exaggeration to say that fallacies "infect" and stymie a huge portion of all daily thinking and discourse.

This strongly suggests the almost unbelievable possibility that learning to recognize and avoid fallacies can be a highly effective remedy and prophylaxis against a general affliction. My own experience with undergraduates is at least anecdotal evidence for this expectation: Students make quantum leaps in their critical thinking after spending only a few days on fallacies. There's marked improvement in oral communication, in on-the-spot thinking, and even in writing—across the curriculum. After studying fallacies, it is hard to tell from their essays that they are still the same students.

THE MOST COMMON FALLACIES

The number of recognized types of fallacies increases yearly as textbook writers recognize and codify new ones. To complicate things a bit, categories overlap here and there. Also, some fallacies have inherently hybrid natures and so enjoy citizenship in more than one category. Despite all this, the classifications for fallacies have, by now, become fairly standard and vastly useful.

For economy of space, we will consider only those fallacies that are most common and most threatening to serious discussion and communication, and these come to nearly two dozen, depending on how we arrange and count them.

So beguiling are the fallacies we have chosen to consider that they deceive even those who commit them. How many of us can, without embarrassment, review the reasoning that went into life-long decisions like the choice of career, lover, spouse, home, diet, friends, number of children? Worse still, the deceptive force of fallacies can take on sinister proportions in the hands of demagogues, dealers, and advertisers who know how well these devices work in mass manipulation and deception. Need one mention the tragic history of this past century to remind us of what a few mad leaders with a talent for verbal demagoguery can do?

In this first chapter on fallacies, we will look at the six that I take to be most deceptive of all. The first four of these seem to come to us most naturally, and are therefore the most common of all. They work by distracting us with irrelevancies and distortions of the subject matter involved. Once we familiarize ourselves with them, however, they become easy to spot or avoid.

RED HERRING: Get Back on the Trail!

The *red herring* fallacy works by introducing a new and irrelevant consideration so as to distract the listener from the real issue. The name "red herring" goes back to the ancient practice of dragging a cured herring across a trail to destroy scent and confuse a team of dogs. Another name for this fallacy is *irrelevant thesis*.

My first confusing encounter with a red herring occurred in the most unlikely of places—a course I was taking as an undergraduate. The person dragging the red herring was the professor. He had just returned our first quiz in which he had misread one of my correct answers and docked me ten points. In a fit of obsessive immaturity—a chronic ailment of mine in those undergraduate days—I tried arguing for my ten points. The professor countered that I would never get through the semester with a perfect average anyway.

He had changed the issue from whether or not I deserved to have the ten points to whether having them would lead to a perfect average by the semester's end. I got sucked in. Instead of staying on track, I argued the new, irrelevant issue by observing that without those ten points, I couldn't possibly finish the semester with a perfect average. I caved in by easily conceding that, even with the ten points, a perfect average was unlikely. With this, the whole matter somehow seemed settled.

As another example, imagine someone arguing against a proposal for some new kind of course and making the following quip: "Are we going to clutter our curriculum with every new fad that comes our way or are we going to hold the line on solid, traditional education?" The speaker attempts to divert attention from the genuine issue of whether the proposed course has merit.

The distracting issue is the trivial one of whether to go with every new fad. On this latter question there would surely be no doubt about favoring a traditional policy over the extreme of recklessly going for every fad that comes along.

As our next example, read the following conversation:

JOAN: American society is by far the greatest in the world. But don't you think it would be still greater if, by every possible legislative, executive, and juridical act, we made sure to guarantee—even more than we have so far—the full rights of every woman in the country?

JON: Your constant obsession with rights amazes me, Joan. Any sociologist will surely tell you that what you're recommending will never result in any perfectly ideal society.

Jon's diversionary issue is whether or not guaranteeing full rights to every American woman would ever yield a perfectly ideal society. Joan is asking a very different question, however, namely, whether guaranteeing full rights for every woman would result in a better society, even if not an ideal one. Jon's answer, which implicitly rejects Joan's recommendation, may seem convincing at first because it expresses a very plausible doubt about whether what Joan wants will yield an ideal society. But a moment's reflection easily tells us that his claim, plausible though it may be, has no bearing at all on the question of whether equal rights would make for a better society.

Here's one, some versions of which you've probably heard many times:

BERT: Harry, Don't you think it would be better for you to smoke outside instead of here in the office?

HARRY: Secondary smoke is no worse than the diesel exhaust of the idling pick-up trucks at our front door every morning. The fumes once made me so sick I had to go to the nearest emergency room.

Harry is obviously dragging a red herring. True, diesel fumes can be harmful, but the issue is whether it would be better for the others if Harry went outside to do his smoking and not whether diesel fumes are worse than secondary smoke.

Now for a red herring that was probably committed more unwittingly:

> Aren't our protectionist trade policies cruel to developing countries like Gambia, the Ivory Coast, Costa Rica, and others around the world, whose fragile economies are critically dependent on exporting produce and raw materials? These countries, for example, most of whose inhabitants are employed in agriculture, cannot afford the gene technology which we protect jealously and which is becoming monopolized by the giant agrochemical companies of the developed world.

> I don't understand how our trade policy can be considered cruel when it is so necessary for protecting some of our faltering industries.

The second speaker is diverting his own attention as well as his companion's from the issue of whether our trade policies are cruel to developing countries. His claim that our protectionism yields us some benefits, though quite acceptable, is irrelevant to the issue that worries the other.

In the way of still another example, I recall hearing countless times that air travel fatalities are far less frequent (relatively speaking) than those caused by autos. For many who are uneasy about flying, though, these arguments are only slimly relevant and, therefore, don't quite cut the mustard. For them, the more central issue is not survival but the probable duration of air-trouble scenarios. An impending disaster can be a torturing experience for the airborne traveler, lasting from seconds to hours. Those well-meaning safety reports may therefore amount to unintended "red herrings" for some of us ground-huggers.

How about the impassioned prosecutor who tells the jury how heinous the crime is when, instead, she should be proving that the defendant did it? Or the politician who attempts to dampen our concerns about some of our most tragic medical ills like AIDS by reminding us of other serious ones like cancer?

Now, how does a red herring so easily distract us? Simply by means of two devices:

1. The irrelevant thesis is superficially similar to the original one. This is what makes it so distracting. The attention easily and unwittingly jumps track to another issue.

2. The irrelevant thesis is always a "very sensible" one on which the author easily wins full agreement. This not only helps distract the listener, but, much more than this, it helps lull him into thinking that the original issue has also been settled. The superficial similarity between the original and the substituted thesis is crucial in creating this illusion.

Operating with features like these, the red herring is one of the most insidious and frequently used instruments of disruption and deception. Every effort, therefore, should be made by the critical thinker to guard against its thwarting rhetorical force. The sharpest and most effective response is the simple retort: True, but irrelevant!

THE FALSE DILEMMA

An executive at a board meeting of a pharmaceutical firm argues that because of a patent expiration and the arrival of generics, the company must either cut the price of a certain drug or else face reduced sales. In doing this the executive has presented a *dilemma*. The argument is a dilemma because the two alternatives it concludes with are both undesirable to the company. Every dilemma concludes, as it were, with two "sharp horns" between which we cannot choose without being scathed by one or the other of them.

The dilemma is *false* if there are in fact alternatives other than the two the dilemma offers. Another executive at the above meeting, for example, might try to "jump between the horns of the dilemma" by suggesting that the company could instead improve certain aspects of quality in this name brand, and possibly, the marketing.

The false dilemma is one of the most disarming of all the fallacies. This is unsurprising, for, when faced with a pair of dire alternatives, we easily overlook the intermediate possibilities. The alternatives are usually extreme ones, and this, of course, adds to their force and distractive power. The fallacy, therefore, works with virtually no felt violence to anyone's good logical sense. As a result, it can leave us all—speaker and audience—impaled on "horns" that have, so to speak, been set too close together.

To avoid false dilemmas, it helps to keep in mind that black/white thinking—no grey area—is usually a case of coarse reasoning and oversimplification. When we engage in it, we risk being charged with simplistic thinking or even with simple-mindedness.

Some of the following examples will have a familiar ring:

MOTHER: Bob, must you flood your room with all that light? You have almost half a kilowatt burning, and you never turn off lights when you leave. Anybody but you would have to use sunglasses in your room. Besides, our energy bill has gone through the ceiling. You do have the reading lamp Uncle Josh gave you, and it's close enough to both your chair and your bed, isn't it?

BOB: Mom, what do you want me to do, stumble around by candlelight?

How much light can Bob cut down without getting lost in the shadows?

We are burning too much gas and must therefore reduce drastically the size of our pleasure cars, even if they aren't as safe as the ones we now drive.

Aren't more fuel-efficient engines a possibility?

LAURA: Tim dear, the doctor said that you must eat less by at least 20 percent. You're dangerously overweight. Besides, you're going to have to drag your excess weight, all eighty pounds of it, to Europe next summer along with the rest of our dead luggage.

TIM: Come on, Laura! What does he expect me to do, starve myself to death?

Can Tim shrink each meal by one-fifth without starving to death?

If you think oil is a pollutant, try burning coal or wood.

How have the other energy alternatives such as natural gas, geothermal, oceanic, solar, and wind been eliminated?
A two-party kind of false dilemma:

From the left:
    The U.S. has the highest crime rate in the world and we ought to do something about it. Let us build more schools, not more jails. The only way to fight crime is to fight poverty and ignorance and the way to do this is to spend more on education.

From the right:
    Yes, our rising crime rate is one of our most urgent problems. We are not tough enough on criminals. Many felons are released too soon in order to make room in our jails. Others are not jailed to begin with. The way to deal with this crisis is to build more jails so as to make punishment longer and more certain. We must make it absolutely clear to our would-be offenders that crime just doesn't pay.

In this discussion, the speakers falsely assume that the two approaches they recommend are mutually exclusive, i.e., that if you have one, you cannot have the other. How about the possibility of using the two approaches together? The amount of available money of course may be a problem, but such a limitation would have to be demonstrated convincingly in terms of budget priorities.

Something like the following clothing ad appeared recently in the magazine section of the *New York Times*:

> Which would you rather see your boys in:
> Jail
> The principal's office
> A pickle
> or
> Our Sahara Club clothes?

Obviously, there are endless other alternatives to the ones mentioned as, for example, some other brand of clothing. This ad is a more general form of false dilemma since it spans more than two alternatives. We might call it a false multilemma.

False dilemmas can be flaky:

HARRY: Okay, Meg, if you had a choice, would you have opted to be born intelligent or good looking?

MEG: I never had that choice, Harry, but having to live with you, I should have been be born stupid instead of good looking.

It is Harry who is committing the false dilemma. Meg is merely juggling alternatives in order to jump immodestly between the "horns" of Harry's false dilemma.

TWO WRONGS: Worse Than One Wrong

We have all, at some time or other, nodded politely when a bore across the way has reminded us that "two wrongs don't make a right any more than two rights make a wrong." Yet what this cliché maxim cautions us against is one of the most seductive and freely committed of all the fallacies. Like the red herring and the false dilemma, the *two wrongs* fallacy works by distracting us. We commit it when we try to minimize a wrong by calling attention to another, usually similar, often worse, wrong.

What makes it so comfortable to commit this fallacy is that it entrances us into sweet inaction. Two wrongs is the cop-out fallacy. Why concern ourselves with some wrong that has just been brought to our attention when there is another wrong, possibly a worse one, that goes uncorrected? Why not do what is easier—simply slither away from the first wrong and bemoan the second one?

Two wrongs is also a consolation fallacy. Afflicted with an acknowledged injustice, however oppressive, we can always find a worse one to console and distract us from the obligation to act on the acknowledged one.

This beguiling fallacy takes several forms, each based on a sightly different mode of appeal.

The Abusive Form

> MOM: Sue, I will not have you talking to me like that. I am your mother, and don't you ever forget it!
>
> SUE: But, Mom, how about the way you talk to Grandma?
>
> SUE'S SISTER: Now wait a sec, Sue. Mom's manners with Grandma may be wrong, but how does that make what you did right? Do two wrongs make a right?

Sue's sister's response is of course cliché but on target. If discourtesy toward one's parents is wrong, then of course Mom's conduct is wrong, but citing Mom's wrongdoing in no way mitigates the wrongness of Sue's actions. Indeed, the inference would seem to go quite the other way around. If, as Sue insists, Mom's manners with Grandma are wrong, then Sue might well concede that her own manners are wrong too. After all, she is doing the very same sort of thing she accuses her mom of doing.

Why does Sue resort to this two wrongs strategy? Why is her fallacious argument so compelling? The answer lies in the fact that she is charging hypocrisy: How can you, Mom, object to what I am doing if, in essence, you have been doing the very same thing? If Sue can make her charge stick, it can distract considerably from the wrongness of her own conduct.

In any case, hypocritical or not, Mom's conduct has little or no bearing on the rightness or wrongness of Sue's conduct. Sue's charge is therefore a diversionary, personally abusive attack.

The "So What?" Form

We commit a second form of the two wrongs fallacy when we attempt to mitigate a wrong by calling attention to other wrongs that are being committed—wrongs against which there is presumably insufficient objection. The other wrongs are more or less similar to the wrong we are fallaciously defending, but they are generally seen by us as more serious. Indeed, the more serious the cited wrongs, the greater the distractive, deceptive impact of the fallacy we are committing.

> A: Do you remember that Joe Camel ad in which the camel's snout was downright obscene? The Reynolds Tobacco Company ought not to have done that sort of thing. I applaud all those who, at the time, made their objections known.

> B: Oh, come on. How about the violence and other more explicit obscenities on TV or at the movie houses? What are we doing about them?

> A: There ought to be more law enforcement on cocaine abuse. There's just too much of it. Bus drivers and even airplane pilots are doing it at great risk to passengers. It's scary.

> B: You're worrying about the wrong substance. There is much more abuse of alcohol than the total of cocaine and all other drugs combined. Alcohol is legal, much cheaper, and probably a greater threat to peace and safety.

In both these examples, the force of the rhetoric is diversionary. It diverts attention from the wrong conduct under consideration to a second, allegedly worse one. The purpose, obviously, is to soften the case against the first wrong.

Calling attention to a greater wrong is an irrelevant, though powerful, psychological move that works by contrasting two effects. We can make any color fade by placing it in a background of greater intensity. This "So what? There are worse things" form of the two wrongs fallacy therefore, is a beguiling strategy that can stifle initiative and action on even the most urgent matters.

By now, you may have noticed that some of these examples might have been easily classified as red herrings which, as you may recall, work by distracting us with a second issue. This, however, should not surprise us. The fallacy categories that have developed over the years do tend to overlap, giving some fallacies dual or near-dual citizenship. We tend to reserve the two wrongs category, however, for issues that are more narrowly about some specific kinds of human conduct, rather than about broader ills.

The Retaliatory Form

For still another form of the two wrongs fallacy we go to the timeworn melodrama in which the husband finds out his wife has been unfaithful and then feels free to have a retaliatory affair of his own.

The force of this fallacy stems from the idea that the victim of any wrong is justified in retaliating with a similar wrong, and that the perpetrator of the first wrong deserves what his former victim is now doing in retaliation. To illustrate how far this form of the two wrongs fallacy can take us, imagine an individual who has had his wallet stolen and, in a fit of blind retaliation, has no qualms about shoplifting or stealing elsewhere in order to recoup his losses.

Let's keep in mind, here, that, generally speaking, the wrongness of the primary act has no direct or simple bearing on the rightness or wrongness of the retaliatory one. Any retaliation is fallacious when it overlooks this. The moral status of a retaliatory act must be judged on grounds that are far more complex than any tit-for-tat strike.

Of course, we sometimes retaliate in order to prevent a worse act. A person or a group being attacked or even threatened may, with some justification, counterattack for ultimate self-defense. The retaliatory act, taken by itself, may be quite violent and destructive. But in such a case, we might be able to argue convincingly that submitting to further aggression and imperiling our survival is worse than retaliating. We therefore choose "the lesser of two evils."

The danger, however, is that the retaliation may be too excessive. The tendency is to over-react and do more harm than is necessary. For this reason the law is careful to admonish against "excessive force" in subduing any perpetrator. You don't shoot the homeless man who curses you when you refuse his window wash even if he kicks your car as you ride off. Indeed, the law insists on due process and on codifying its penalties so as to avoid the "cruel and excessive" punishment that would then count as a second wrong.

Some students of the subject are against retaliatory justice, altogether. They call it retributive justice. These theorists believe that rehabilitation and education as preventative and corrective measures are the more effective ways of dealing with crime. According to them, therefore, a punitive policy which deprives persons of life or liberty is institutionalized vengeance on the part of society. It simply heaps wrong upon wrong unless we can show, conclusively, that it is the *only* way of deterring people from committing more wrongs.

The Everybody-Does-it Form

AGNES: Myra, should you be taking that computer paper home for your personal use?

MYRA: It's okay, Agnes. Around here they all avail themselves of some company supplies now and then.

Petty theft on the part of employees costs American industry hundreds of millions of dollars yearly and has contributed heavily to the failures of many businesses. Federal, state, and local tax dollars lost to the underground economy go into the high billions. Yet, how many of us can firmly claim to stand outside the protective shade of the two wrongs umbrella on these issues?

A Fast Play on Two Wrongs

A: Why worry about petty thieving? It may be wrong, but it's far better than armed robbery.

B: Okay. So let's always do the better thing. We'll go for petty thieving instead of armed robbery.

Obviously, there are a number of things wrong with the messy reasoning in this conversation.

APPEAL TO AUTHORITY:
Modesty Is Not Always the Best Policy

This is the fourth of our diversionary fallacies and the one we fall into so naturally that there is probably no functioning individual who has not committed it.

The fallacy works by appealing to authority to bolster a position in cases where it is possible to argue more relevantly from the inherent merits of the position. By referring to the authority we distract from the fact that the more relevant considerations have not been provided.

The Latin name for this type of fallacy is *argumentum ad verecundiam* (*verecundus* is Latin for "modesty with shame"). The idea is that in committing this fallacy we are yielding to those we think are more knowledgeable. The authority we appeal to does not have to be any particular individual; it can be groups or even a whole tradition.

Appealing to an Individual

Early in this century, when psychical research was a subject of great interest, an editor once commented that "There must be something to psychical research if famous scientists like Jeans and Eddington take it so seriously."

Appealing to a Group

Two million dogs have switched to Alpo.

Appealing to a Tradition

In every society of record, there has been some belief in a god or gods. Therefore, there must be something to theism and religion.

Recall one of our examples in chapter 1 where we mentioned that a grossly wrong value for the earth's circumference, calculated in antiquity, led Columbus, seventeen centuries later, to think he had reached the Orient. No doubt, this incorrect value was originally accepted by some individual in authority. Fallaciously appealing to this authority then made it a matter of tradition. Finally, on the authority of this tradition, those who believed the earth was round—Columbus among them—fallaciously continued to accept the incorrect value. This was, of course, a case of authority operating in two ways: first, by way of an individual, later, by tradition.

For an interesting variant of the fallacy we have been discussing, consider the following astounding but actual occurrence.

Mystification

During a recently aired panel discussion, a very powerful congressman was asked why the federal government was moving toward yielding federal control of water quality to the states. It was pointed out that some rivers run through several states and that what one state does can affect drinking water in another state. The law-maker countered with a specific example about San Diego. He started by vehemently stating that federal controls over San Diego's drinking water were not needed. He then went on to back this up by saying that there had been no problem with the quality of water in San Diego Bay and San Diego had the whole Pacific Ocean at its disposal anyway.

The dozen or so members of the panel seemed to have been left speechless and somewhat dumbstruck. They may have been trying either to recall just what had happened in San Diego or to puzzle out precisely what the whole Pacific Ocean and the water quality in San Diego Bay had to do with San Diego drinking water. The matter was quietly dropped and the discussion ambled on to another subject. The gambit that seems to have been played here is a favorite of many politicians. It consists of responding to a question by citing, authoritatively and in detail, some surprise fact that is either only remotely related to the question or not relevant at all. The intimidating factors are the prominence of the speaker, the authority in his or her manner, insufficient familiarity on the part of the audience with what the speaker is suddenly referring to, and, most of all, the difficulty the audience is having with finding the connection. Unfortunately, under such circumstances the audience often drops the question as though it were settled. The fallacy of course consists in modestly believing (*verecundus*) that the question has somehow been answered when in fact no such thing has even begun to happen.

Certainly, there are times when the level of expertise required to defend a position is so specialized that we cannot profitably benefit from entering into reasoned argument. In such a case, appealing to an authority is no fallacy at all, provided, of course the authority's qualifications are demonstrable and relevant. We routinely go to a lawyer for an issue in law, to a doctor for one in medicine, to a scientist for one in science. In scholarly reading, we go to footnotes. Even so, when we do go to the experts, let's not be too modest. Rarely in routine living is anything hopelessly and totally beyond our comprehension. Were this not so, we'd be stone frozen in most of our decision making. What question of practical concern can possibly be so difficult that all we can ever hope for is an expert's answer, backed not by relevant reasons, but only by his prestige and his credentials? Recall that even some of the most esoteric mathematical and scientific issues have gotten a measure of intelligible "airing" in newspapers and other media vehicles, however vague or general these accounts may have been.

Those counselors, be they teachers, proselytizers, physicians, engineers, or other technical consultants, who cannot offer their audiences some reasons other than their prestige and authority are either arrogant or seriously deficient in their subject. We must ask more of our advisors. We are almost always capable of grasping enough to make some sense of things and are therefore entitled to ask.

NAPOLEON: Giuseppe, what shall we do with this soldier? Everything he says is wrong.

GIUSEPPE: Make him a general, your Excellency, and everything he says will be right.

THE LEADING QUESTION: Divide and Conquer

I remember once sitting in an introductory anatomy class as an observer. At one point in the lecture, the professor reminded the class that whenever we exert muscular effort we sometimes pull things and sometimes push things. He then proceeded to ask if anyone knew which are the muscles that push and which are the ones that pull. After a wave of mumbling flowed through the class, one student, who, I later learned, was switching from law to medicine, said, "Sir, is that a trick question? Are we supposed to assume that some muscles are capable of pulling and others of pushing?" This student had obviously learned his law lessons well. The professor of course replied that muscles, like ropes, can only pull, not push.

The *leading question* fallacy also goes under names like complex question, loaded question, and trick question. It is committed with a faulty question rather than a defective argument. The question is essentially a complex one in that although it is framed as a single question, it also has in it one or more hidden (implied, unasked) questions: "Have you stopped lying to your wife?"

What is faulty about a question of this sort is that it asks for one blanket answer—usually just a "yes" or "no"—to two and sometimes more questions which have separate and possibly different answers. Giving such an answer is like buying a package tour. Some places on the itinerary you truly look forward to, others you could well do without, but in buying the tour you commit yourself to all of it. Similarly, when responding to a complex question with a simple, blanket answer, we commit ourselves, sometimes unwittingly, to answers which we may not wish to give. One can easily see how prosecutors questioning witnesses can resort to this kind of tactic in the hope of getting witnesses to incriminate themselves: "Do you enjoy using crack?" That the witness ever took crack has not yet been established. Yet, the question suggests that she does, and the innuendo persists whether she answers yes or no. Even if she answers in the negative, her answer could be understood to mean that though she uses crack she does not enjoy it. A proper response would be to reject the question and ask the interrogator to divide it into the components he has in mind: (1) Have you ever used crack? (2) (If the answer is yes) Do you enjoy it?

> PROSECUTION: Mr. Hooligan, as in the other occasions that you have taken the witness stand in the course of this case, you seem bleary-eyed and exhausted. Are you still having trouble sleeping at night?
>
> DEFENSE: Objection, your honor. The witness is being asked to answer a leading question.

The defense attorney here is guarding against the suggestion that the defendant is not sleeping enough, possibly because of a guilty conscience. The unasked question whose answer is assumed is "Has the defendant been having trouble sleeping?"

"Are you enraged *very often* by discourteous drivers?"

The unanswered question to which a positive answer has been assumed by the cross-examiner is "Are you enraged by discourteous drivers?" The aim of the prosecutor of course is to trick the defendant into incriminating himself with the implied positive answer.

Although complex questions are used to trick respondents into incriminating themselves, they often arise quite naturally in our discourse, either in a benevolent attempt to make an appeal of some sort or simply as a result of loose or careless thinking: "How many of you kids would like to be good citizens and help clean up the streets in our neighborhood?"

Some of them might like to be good citizens but might not care to help clean up the streets; there may be other ways of being good citizens.

Sometimes a question is complex because it not only asks one question, but in doing so it assumes answers to one or more other questions. In such a case it is more usually called a leading question. An example: "How does handwriting reveal personality?" The two simultaneous questions here are "Does handwriting reveal personality?" and "How so?"

"Can you afford to be embarrassed again by loose dentures?"

This is a truly familiar one in which a dental cream company has assumed positive answers to a cluster of other questions, namely "Do you wear dentures?" "Were you ever embarrassed by loose dentures?" "Do you use dental cream?" "Will you probably be embarrassed again by loose dentures?" and so on.

Our next fallacy is the most deceptive of all. Although in its crudest form, it is trivial and obvious, it can be committed with such subtlety as to make it one of the most delusive forms of sophistry and by far the most difficult to detect or avoid. We go now to question begging.

QUESTION BEGGING: Hollow Thinking

Surely you have at some time encountered an argument which seemed to address the issue, but rang hollow nonetheless. Somehow it managed to dodge or skirt the heart of the issue. Chances are that the author, wittingly or unwittingly, was dusting your eyes with the fallacy of *question begging*. Medieval scholars called this *petitio principii* in order to suggest that the question beggar *begs*, i.e., dodges (evades) the issue under consideration instead of reasoning to a conclusion about it.

Question beggars dodge issues in a variety of ways. For a close up on some of these strategies, let us look at a few examples. Don't be lulled by the triviality and obviousness of these.

Circular Reasoning

> "We ought to have capital punishment because if one takes a life, one must give a life."

This argument is blatantly circular and exemplifies the most elemental form of question begging. Instead of arguing for his thesis, the author simply repeats it as a premise, namely that if you take a life you must give a life. And this, of course, is little more than another version of the claim that we ought to have some form of capital punishment.

For another example, here is my paraphrase of an answer I once heard from a retired officer fielding some questions about military service.

> Q: Why is it illegal for any American woman to serve in combat?

> A: Well, simply because established federal law explicitly prohibits any soldier in the American armed forces, under any circumstance whatever, from serving in combat unless he is an able-bodied, adult male.

Clearly this answer is a cop-out. It goes nowhere toward answering the question, which calls for some reasons for legally excluding women from military combat. Instead of providing the explanation, the respondent merely repeats the very fact of law that he should be justifying, and he does this by disguising the repetition in more elaborate language. In essence, his response comes down to saying: It's illegal for American women to serve in combat because it's illegal for American women to serve in combat. In precisely this manner, he has failed to answer the question by dodging or begging it with empty, circular rhetoric.

Sometimes, this kind of circular reasoning is a little less obvious. Consider for example the following excerpt from a newspaper editorial of several years ago during George Bush's presidency (revised for brevity):

> Despite the fact that the glow of the Gulf War has long faded, the economy is a mess, and Americans are desperate for decent jobs, health care, schools, and housing, George Bush will be re-elected because . . . like Ronald Reagan he is a Teflon President. Even the recession has not dented his popularity.

The author here gives what may at first seem to be a genuine reason for believing that George Bush will be re-elected despite all that is bad with the country. This reason is that he is a "Teflon President." What this picturesque metaphor tells us is that the ills of the nation will not taint or tarnish George Bush's popularity in any way, and this is equivalent to saying that he will, no matter how bad things get, continue to draw a winning vote, which is to say that he will, despite all the ills of the nation, be re-elected. The argument, then, comes to no more than this: George Bush will be re-elected no matter what goes wrong on the domestic scene because he will draw the American vote (i.e., be re-elected), no matter what goes wrong on the domestic scene.

The author has fallen short of the promise that comes with the word "because." His "short-circuited" reasoning amounts to question begging. And the question he has begged is "Why will

Bush be re-elected no matter what goes wrong on the domestic scene?" (Approximately equivalent to: Why will he continue to be very popular with the voters no matter what goes wrong on the domestic scene?)

Conclusion Smuggling

For a more slippery but actually more familiar kind of question begging, consider the following brief dialogue about the existence of UFOs.

> A: How can you believe in UFOs? They're nothing but figments of some vivid imaginations.

> B: Some figments! Just wait until one eventually lands in your backyard. You'll believe in them then.

B has short-changed A. The underlying issue is the existence of UFOs. Instead of arguing for this existence, B expresses some vague likelihood that a UFO will actually land in A's back yard. In doing this, B is indirectly (implicitly) assuming the existence UFOs—the very thing he is supposed to justify rather than smuggle in as a hidden assumption.

Even young children, unable to detect the question begging fallacy, will commit it without qualms:

> BOBBY: Hi, Henry! Do you know who the smartest guy on this block is? It's my father.

> HENRY: You're wrong, because my father is.

The young question beggar here is Henry, and the issue is, is Bobby wrong? True, Bobby makes an unsupported claim, but he is merely bragging dogmatically. Henry, on the other hand, with the term, "because," makes a pretense at "proving" that Bobby is wrong, but he succeeds only in begging this question by gratuitously starting his argument with the debatable, explicit premise that it is his own father who is the smartest. In making this assumption, however, he is essentially (implicitly) assuming that Bobby is wrong. For, obviously, both fathers could not be the one smartest.

A still more subtle maneuver is that of sidestepping: "We all know that murder is wrong, and abortion is murder. Therefore, abortion is wrong."

The underlying issue here is whether abortion is wrong, and this argument begs it. Its author first sidesteps the question by flatly assuming a positive answer to another question, namely, whether abortion is murder. In assuming that answer, the author arbitrarily stacks the cards in his favor, since no one would dispute that murder is wrong. The wrongness of abortion, however, is the very thing he was supposed to establish, not by implicitly assuming it in his sidestep, but by arguing for it. The author, therefore, has engaged in question begging. To escape the fallacy, he might have tried to establish that abortion is murder.

Because question begging is so elusive and deceptive, let's run through a few more examples. Some of the following are obvious, others are a bit tricky. They all work in one or another of the ways we have already discussed.

In denying that God exists you are offending him.

Instead of justifying belief in God, this argument implicitly assumes it by warning about offending Him.

Here is what may be a familiar but trickier example of this elusive sort of question begging:

JON: Why is there so much static in your radio this morning? I rode to work with you yesterday and it sounded fine then.

NEIGHBOR: It's those damn sunspots.

JON: How do you know that?

NEIGHBOR: Come on, Jon, don't you hear the static?

That there is something fallaciously circular about the neighbor's reasoning is obvious to any of us. Just how the fallacy occurs is less evident.

The answer lies in a problematic, implicit premise that the neighbor makes. He tacitly assumes that sunspots are the major cause of static during good weather and in any otherwise well-functioning radio. If we grant the neighbor's assumption, his conclusion that solar disturbances could very well be causing the static is quite plausible. But Jon is essentially challenging the assumption, and it therefore becomes the real issue in question.

The neighbor's answer, however, begs, i.e., avoids confronting, this issue. For, in pointing again to the static, he implicitly reassumes—instead of justifying—his underlying belief that sunspots are the major cause of static in good radios and good weather. This return to his original conclusion seems much too facile. It taints his reasoning with the scent of circularity thus alerting us that something is wrong.

To avoid the circularity, the neighbor would have to offer "outside" evidence for his underlying premise about the cause of sunspots. He might, for example, have quoted a scientific source or even reported that, in the past, he had himself seen unusual amounts of solar activity with his own amateur telescope whenever he had static on his radio. Had he done any of this, his underlying assumption that static is to be associated with sunspots under otherwise normal conditions would, to some extent, have been justified, even if only slightly.

Another tricky one:

> Should same-sex unions be duly licensed and accorded the same economic and civic status as heterosexual marriages?
>
> No, marriage is, by definition, the union of a man and a woman. Same-sex unions violate this definition and therefore should not be given the stamp of approval that goes with licensing.

The respondent has engaged in question begging by tacitly assuming that we should not approve of any union that violates the going definition of marriage. By making this assumption he indirectly (implicitly) assumes that we should not approve same-sex unions. He has therefore implicitly, and probably unwittingly, assumed an answer to the issue instead of offering a genuine argument for the answer.

Question begging can be harmless and amusing whenever it occurs with crude obviousness.

GIG: Why do you keep snapping your fingers, Gag?

GAG: To keep the elephants away.

GIG: I don't see any elephants.

GAG: You see, it works!

Summing up on question begging: We engage in it when we offer a conclusion on an issue by constructing an empty argument instead of a genuine one. The empty argument is typically one in which we inject or smuggle into our premises the very conclusion we favor. In the "smuggling" operation, we often camouflage the contraband by either rewording it beyond easy recognition or by hiding it within the folds of some broader assumption.

Our desired conclusion then must, of course, follow necessarily from our trumped-up premises. For certainly, a conclusion cannot fail to follow validly from premises that already include it. The whole construction, however, is nothing more than empty self-justification that casts no light whatever on the issue in question.

The self-justifying element in question begging has deservedly earned the label of circular reasoning. This geometric metaphor brings out the fact that the conclusion "cycles" from desired conclusion to premises to conclusion again thereby trivializing the entire notion of argument according to which one is supposed to justify a claim (conclusion) by means of another firmly acceptable claim serving as a reason or premise. The striking feature of question begging is that, depending on how subtly it is constructed, it can be extraordinarily convincing and therefore deceptive. The author appears to have given reasons for her conclusion when, instead, she has essentially only assumed it.

It seems fair to say, however, that, despite its highly elusive and deceptive potential, question begging is a fallacy that we are more likely to commit unwittingly than by design. It is not easy to invent arguments in which we assume the very conclusions we are supposed to be "proving" and do it cleverly enough to get away with it.

Nevertheless in the course of reasoning, subtle question begging errors are easily made as we quite naturally reach out to embrace some parts or all of our conclusions even before we have amply justified them. As a result, this mind-numbing fallacy is extremely widespread despite its subtleness and usually innocent origins. Developing a sensitive nose for it, therefore, will most certainly sharpen and sophisticate our critical responses both to our own thinking and to that of others.

*   *   *

Having discussed six of the most deceptive kinds of bad reasoning, we go on to our next chapter where we take up two types of fallacies that work not only by distraction but also by abuse. One of them abuses the author of an opposed point of view, the other abuses the argument. Both can be very damaging put-downs.

9

ABUSE:
Crude and Damaging

PERSONAL ABUSE

Personal abuse is the most common and crudest of the fallacies—
also the most damaging. Fortunately, it is the easiest to recognize, but
the harm it does is difficult to neutralize. The offensiveness of this fallacy makes it, probably, more disruptive than all the others put
together. Its Latin name, the *ad hominem* fallacy, expresses the idea
that the attack is aimed at the person rather than at the argument.

To commit the fallacy, simply ignore the issue and attack the
speaker. Attack irreverently and even abusively; ridicule him if
possible. How can you go wrong? We're all vulnerable. Just
dream up some possible fault or hidden agenda. Whether or not
the speaker has it matters little. Just plaster him with it, preferably in the presence of others. Do this and the emotional turmoil
you'll set off will render your victim incapable of the slightest
comeback. A foul enough onslaught can leave him defensive and
helpless for some time to come.

114

If someone does any of this to you, it could spark off a rush of rage (justified, of course), but don't lose your cool. The best retaliation is the unreactive one. Ignore it and go on with what you were doing. The seaminess of the attack eventually shows itself to virtually all observers.

Here are some examples that should ring familiar:

Not many years ago, a prominent U.S. senator, during a debate on the Equal Rights Amendment, dismissed feminists as "a band of bra-less bubbleheads."

A congressman from one of the timber-rich states once described environmentalists as "screwed up visionaries who favor the spotted owl above the welfare of the families that depend on jobs in the lumbering industry."

On evolution: The theory of evolution is a false doctrine propounded by a group of absurd and amoral atheists who expect us to believe that our ancestors were sea slime animals.

From a recent juror: "I wouldn't buy any argument those prosecutors give. They'll say anything just to get a conviction."

SAM: What did the doctor prescribe for your chest pains?

MOLLY: Eight aspirin tablets per day for five days. He said I have costa chondritis, and the aspirin, which is anti-inflammatory, will probably do the job.

SAM: Do you think you should be taking all those aspirins? I happen to know he's heavily invested in the Bayer Company.

Ad hominem arguments are not always crude. Spiro Agnew once smoothly dismissed his intellectual opponents as: "an effete corps of impudent snobs who characterize themselves as intellectuals."

A: Why was that nice fellow, Jim, suddenly fired?

B: His supervisor reported that he was found drinking on the job. I happen to know the supervisor, though, and let me tell you—he has a particularly strong dislike of Cuban immigrants. Jim is one, and the supervisor got rid of him.

Imagine that Jim files with his labor union's grievance committee, claiming that he was fired because of prejudice. In such a case, the immediate and relevant concerns of the committee are the reasons that the supervisor gave for firing him. And these would no doubt be about Jim's drinking on the job. A discriminatory feeling against Cubans or even just a personal dislike may have been there all along, but citing such motives cannot figure in the justification of the dismissal. Only facts about Jim's performance and general conduct in the workplace can do that.

The grievance committee may find that the supervisor's report is accurate and that Jim's conduct violates fair rules and possibly safety standards. This, then, would surely count toward justifying dismissal. If the committee finds such allegations to be untrue, then Jim's firing lacks justification.

Finding no justification for Jim's dismissal, the grievance committee may then wish to go further. It may want to explain (not justify) the dismissal. In other words, the committee may seek to discover why Jim was dismissed, what motives, attitudes, preferences, or other emotional states moved the supervisor to recommend the dismissal. This would throw light on the dynamics or play of forces underlying Jim's dismissal, and it could be useful especially if some law or standard of fairness had been breached and prosecution of the supervisor was in order.

On an interpretation that some would consider uncharitable, one might find a touch of the *ad hominem* even in so venerable an authority as Scripture: "Let him who is without sin cast the first stone."

The casting of a stone is, of course, an act of condemnation against the defendant, who, in the story, happens to be the alleged adulteress, Mary Magdalene. The passage may then be understood to be saying that only one who is free of infractions may sit in judgment of another. Under such a standard, could any of us ever hope to qualify? Similarly, during the historic hearings several years ago on the Supreme Court nominee Clarence Thomas, some Americans objected to the inclusion of Senator Edward Kennedy on the panel that asked the questions. They disapproved on the basis of how they saw the senator's conduct in his own private life.

The rhetorical force of requiring that one who judges and condemns another be himself a person of integrity is considerable. To begin with, it does violence to our sense of fairness to allow someone with a blemished personal history to sit in judgment of others. He simply doesn't deserve the distinction. (It is perhaps to this standard that the scriptural admonition is appealing.)

Also, one who judges and condemns is implicitly saying: "You ought not do that sort of thing," and this, of course, would mark the judge with a tainted past as an untrustworthy hypocrite whose own conduct does not match what he preaches. True—we would like to trust those who are to judge us. This is why we ask for such background items as professional licenses and character references. It is reasonable to want that extra assurance. But primarily, it is the reasoning or justification behind any judgment that we must validate and not the author of the judgment. When the reasoning is technically beyond us, we do best to enlist the elucidations of those who know enough about the subject matter at issue.

THE LEGAL AD HOMINEM

Attacking the author of a claim is certainly not fallacious in a court of law. An attorney may quite properly test the credibility of any witness—and for two reasons. First of all, legal testimony is often not an argument, but only a report from a witness who has sworn to tell the truth. The sincerity and competency of the witness is therefore entirely relevant and so may be properly brought into question. Second, if the testimony of an expert is an argument, it may be too advanced or too technical for the nonspecialist jury member to follow. For example, the reliability of a psychologist who in the past has been convicted of perjury or who spends more time testifying in courts than working at his profession might be seriously questioned.

STRAW MAN: Let Him Fall, and Then Go On

And now, for the fallacy which abuses not the author of an argument but the argument itself. We commit it when we weaken an opponent's position by distorting it. The misrepresentation then, like a straw man, is either easily "knocked over" or made to look altogether ridiculous.

Those who commit the *straw man* fallacy do it in a variety of ways:

- They may over-simplify or over-complicate and thus over-burden an opponent's claim.
- They may take the claim out of context or read it too literally.
- They may simply burlesque or ridicule it.

Let us illustrate each of these strategies:

OVER-SIMPLIFYING

Why are you all for the study of Greek and Latin? They're dead and useless languages.

This oversimplification distorts by failing to recognize that a rich literature exists in these languages and that they make up large portions of many modern languages, including English.

OVER-BURDENING

Feminists want to abolish all sexual differences.

For the purposes of argument, the antifeminist here is over-burdening the feminist thesis by distortively suggesting that the aim of feminism is to obliterate all differences between the sexes, possibly even physical ones. We might note that, by raising the question of whether all other differences should (or can) be abolished, the author is diverting attention from the central issue in feminism—namely, the differences of opportunity between the sexes.

TAKING OUT OF CONTEXT

You want to ban capital punishment because it entails killing. Then, why not ban eating? After all, it also entails killing—the killing of plants and animals.

This argument takes the issue out of proper context where the term "killing" refers only to the taking of a human life, and not of any other form.

READING TOO LITERALLY

Pam, a teenager, is pleading with her mother to let her go to the beach party after the baseball game next weekend:

PAM: I really want to go, Mom. All my friends are going. Please let me!

MOTHER: How many of you are going?

PAM: Ten, besides myself.

MOTHER: Well then, not *all* your friends are going. You have more than ten friends. Don't you? At least fifteen, no?

PAM: Oh, Mom, you know what I mean.

Pam tries again:

PAM: Okay Mom, but can I go to the big rock concert in New York next month right after school closes? Everyone's mother is letting her kids go.

MOTHER: I'm not everyone's mother.

RIDICULING

Someone making a pitch against bilingual education:

> Okay, should every other sentence or every other word be English?

* * *

Imagine how messy reasoning can get when we play fast and loose with word meanings. Let's see how some of this happens—in our next chapter.

10

DOUBLE TALK:
Stay Single

AMBIGUITY

We all know the "sound" of double talk or ambiguity—when we cannot tell, from context, which of two or more meanings a speaker or writer has in mind. This happens in two ways. One is uncertainty in how the author is using some key word or phrase. Logicians call the ambiguity it causes *semantic ambiguity* or equivocation. The other is loose grammar, and the resulting ambiguity is known as *syntactic ambiguity* or *amphiboly*. Ambiguity, though often detrimental to communication, is not in itself fallacious. We commit a fallacy as soon as we allow ambiguity to flaw or "infect" our arguments.

EQUIVOCATION

The equivocator uses a word or phrase differently, i.e., with a different meaning, at different places in an argument. In this way, he shifts without warning from one meaning to another in order to secure some desired conclusion. The fallacy is deceptive because, if we do not take the change of meaning into account, the argument appears to be (and in fact is) at least formally correct:

> Man alone is rational.
> No woman is a man.
> *Therefore*
> No woman is rational.

In this silly example, the word "man" refers to all humans in the first premise, and to only male humans in the second premise. The argument equivocates on the word "man."

A more serious example is the sort of argument some have given in order to shield smoking from the charge that it causes cancer.

> We do not know what causes cancer.
> *Therefore*
> We cannot say that smoking causes cancer.

This argument equivocates on the term "cause." In the premise, the term is used in the sense of *basic cause* as, for example, some biological mechanism, possibly on the cellular level, which would explain precisely how anyone gets cancer. In this sense of "cause" it is true that we do not yet quite know "the cause." In the conclusion, however, "cause" does a very different sort of semantic "job." There, it has the sense of *contributory cause*.

To see this, suppose we were to disagree with the conclusion. What would we then be saying? Simply that there are good grounds for believing that smoking contributes significantly to the likelihood of getting cancer and, in this sense, is a (contributory) cause of cancer, even if we cannot specify the exact physiologic pathways by which this happens.

Here is an argument that a Chinese official recently gave to defend the Beijing government against the charge that it tyrannizes its people:

> The People's Republic of China is a democracy.
> No democracy ever tyrannizes its people.
> *Therefore*
> The government of China never tyrannizes its people.

The equivocation here is on the term "democracy." In the first premise the speaker uses "democracy" to maintain (rightly or wrongly) that the government of China is a government of the working class comprising the vast majority of the Chinese people. In the second premise, however, "democracy" is burdened with additional work. There it is made to convey the sense of a government committed to human rights such as freedom of speech and assembly.

With the proper semantic adjustments, each of the premises, as independent claims, seems plausible. They cannot both serve in the same argument, however, because the "democracy" of the first premise is not the same as the "democracy" of the second. Another way of putting this is to say that the term "democracy" cannot serve as a connecting term in the argument because its meaning has changed.

A rather common and very subtle example of the fallacy of ambiguity is one which equivocates rather elusively on the term "right." With rising consciousness of what it is to be a "human right," this form of the fallacy has become so common that it merits some special attention:

NEW NEIGHBOR: Hi there, just want to ask whether my landscapers can step briefly onto your property. They will be planting a rather large Russian spruce—on my side of the line of course.

OLD RESIDENT: No, I wouldn't mind your men standing on my property, but I am dismayed with your plans. Russian spruces produce a yellow powder in the fall that I am deathly allergic

to. Besides, you will be putting a large tree close to where, as
you can see, I grow my vegetables. It is the only sunny spot I
have for growing things, and the shade of your tree will put an
end to it all. In view of the fact that on the other side it would
look as good and also provide you, instead of me, with the
shade, wouldn't it be better or "more right" to plant it there
instead of here?

NEW NEIGHBOR: I'm very sorry, but I have a perfect right to
plant my tree wherever I please on my property, and no one is
going to tell me otherwise!

The new neighbor is essentially equivocating on the term
"right." His flawed argument, expressed more explicitly, may be
paraphrased:

> I am within my "rights" in planting my tree wherever I please
>   on my property.
> *Therefore*
> I am "right" in planting my tree wherever I please on my property.

A similar equivocation occurs in the following version of a
true story of not too long ago:

COMMENTATOR: Wasn't it wrong for a great entertainer like you
to have recorded such an inciting song? Your audience consists
of mostly teenagers and the message in your recording is
nothing but a clarion call to violence.

ENTERTAINER: Sir, this is a free country. I am an artist with a
perfect right to speak my mind. And the First Amendment of
our Constitution secures this right for everyone. Would you
want to deprive me of it?

COMMENTATOR: I certainly would not want to deprive you of
any right, and I'm certainly glad we have that First Amendment to protect it. You do have a right to say the things you
said in your song. But is it right for you to have in fact said
those things? How does having a right to, make it right to?

A SERIOUS MISUNDERSTANDING

The reasoning error in these "rights" examples stems from a serious misunderstanding which has become more and more common as the media and the world of art have increasingly freed themselves of traditional taboos and given expression to subject matter that was once considered inappropriate for some audiences. The "right" which our entertainer speaks of is a freedom—in this case, freedom of expression. It is a right in the sense that no one can legally prevent anyone from saying what she wants to say.

As our first example indicates, freedom of expression is not the only freedom which our laws protect. I have a right to quit my job; lie to my spouse; choose my friends, neighborhood, career; spend all my money in gambling casinos; publish racist slogans; and do all sorts of things in "the pursuit of happiness." But having these freedoms by no means implies that exercising them on any particular occasion is the *right* thing to do. The rightness of my choices is a matter of ethics and must be decided on moral rather than legal grounds. These are grounds that are very different from that of having the legal freedom to choose. Careful attention to this difference can, these days, save much energy and time in reasoned discourse.

Freedom and rightness have been confused even in the most unexpected places. In a recent verbal skirmish on the House of Representatives floor, a prominent congressman was accused by an opposed colleague of having used his speaking privileges in Congress to promote one of his own personal (marketable) products and thus having acted for personal profit and therefore improperly. The accused congressman retorted that what he did was perfectly okay because congressional representatives had always had the right to say anything they wanted on the House floor. The long dispute which followed might have been shortened considerably had someone, at the time, simply pointed out that the disputants were looking at two separate issues—the right to say something and the rightness of saying it—and that the first of these had insufficient bearing on the second.

The careful categorizer of fallacies might easily object here that these last three accounts are not really good examples of equivocation, because, despite the fact that the word "right" taken by itself, does occur in two senses, the actual terms involved in the reasoning are quite different. They are "having the right to" and "being right in."

Strictly speaking, this objection has some point. We could have taken the argument:

> I have a right to do x.
> *Therefore*
> I am right in doing x.

to be a case of plain irrelevancy; since the premise has no bearing on the conclusion. But the fact that "right" does occur in both phrases, with altered partial meaning, as it were, does invest such an argument with an element of deceptive ambiguity. Indeed, it is the occurrence of one and the same word, i.e., "right," in both contexts, that gives these fallacious arguments their aura of plausibility. On the basis of these considerations, our examples might be better characterized as red herrings: They do operate by introducing a new issue (one of rights) in order to distract from the issue at hand (one of ethics), which is quite different despite the superficial but deceptive similarity produced by the recurrence of the word "right." Once again, we have here a fallacy—and we will encounter others—which can be placed under more than one category.

AMPHIBOLY: More Fun Than Deception

Amphiboly arises from loose grammatical structure, i.e., from what we've called syntactic ambiguity. Few of us ever really stumble on it, but it does serve to make us laugh when we do.

Indeed, in most of Gracie Allen's humor the driving force was syntactic ambiguity.

The following are some amusing and perhaps familiar examples, not of actual arguments that commit amphiboly, but of passages which contain syntactic ambiguities and which, if used as premises, would result in fallacious arguments with (possibly) troublesome conclusions.

> Wanted: A college senior for cooking.

> Roadhouse sign: Clean and Decent Dancing Every Night Except Sunday.

> Dog ad: Eats everything. Very fond of children.

> School notice: There will be a lecture on sexual misconduct in the auditorium.

A jailer in Siberia received the following communique from the czar:

> Pardon impossible to be executed

The jailer read it as though there was a period after the word "Pardon" and released the prisoner. The period, however, was meant to be after the word "impossible." It is not known what became of the jailer. The czar, not caring much about "unequals" being substituted for "unequals," may have substituted the jailer for the prisoner.

Pronouns, especially "it" and "them," and words like "any" can be very troublesome when their antecedents (the things they refer to) are unclear.

> Mother said: "Be sure to take the cat out of the bath water before throwing it out the back window."

> Some escaped prisoners are being sought in these parts by several guards. If you spot any, signal us immediately.

The sergeant: "Hold the hand grenade firmly, and pull out the pin. Then throw it as far as you can."

It is unsurprising that our English teachers never tired of correcting for remote antecedents!

The confusion due to fallacies can always put us in harm's way. In our next chapter we take up the most dangerous ones.

11

A LITTLE KNOWLEDGE . . . :
Your Life on the Line

FALSE CAUSE:
The Most Dangerous Game in Town!

Knowing the causes of things not only deepens our understanding, it also enables us to make things happen as opposed to
just letting them happen. Although discovering causes is one of
the most natural and practical of human activities, it is one of the
most difficult. In our hurry to know what is causing the events
around us, we often jump to conclusions. If this happens and it
turns out right, we're lucky. We've escaped the proverbial danger
of "a little knowledge." The fallacy we have committed is one of
several types that fall under the category of *false cause*. These
very dangerous fallacies are also called *non causa pro causa*,
which is latin for "a non-cause (mistaken) for a cause."

It will be helpful to keep in mind that the fallacies we're discussing are variants of one basic type, namely, false cause, and
that they are therefore very closely related.

SIMPLE SUCCESSION: Too Simple

The fallacy of *simple succession* is the crudest form of the false cause fallacy. These examples will seem familiar:

> TOM: Glad you're back, Pam. You seem to have finally gotten over your cold.
>
> PAM: Yeah. Last night just before I went to bed, I took a large glassful of hot tea with cognac. I should have done it a week ago when I first started to sniffle.

Pam obviously thinks that drinking hot tea and cognac cured her cold.

> A few weeks after a recent eclipse of the sun in Mexico an avocado tree lost its leaves and some of its unripe fruit. The owner blamed "eclipse rays" for the damage.
>
> It has been said that the natives of the West Indies brought Columbus food he needed badly because he had assured them during an eclipse that daylight would return in a matter of minutes, and, of course, it did. Apparently the natives thought that Columbus in some way caused the sun to come out again.
>
> The fact that lightning precedes thunder has led many observers to believe that lightning causes thunder. Meteorologists tell us, however, that we are on better grounds when we say not that lightning causes thunder, but that both are caused by a third event, namely a discharge of electricity.

All these examples illustrate the fallacy of simple succession, and we commit it by concluding that because A precedes B, A causes B. The Latin name of this fallacy is *post hoc ergo propter hoc,* which means, literally, "after the thing therefore because of the thing."

Simple succession is the most common form of the false cause fallacy. We have all indulged in it at some time or other, and the closer the two events, A and B, are in time, the more likely we are to commit the fallacy and to be persuaded by it.

Simple succession is a not fallacy because events that succeed each other in time cannot be causally related. They certainly can be and often are. The idea, however, is that simple succession alone is not reason enough to conclude that there is a causal relation at work. The fallacy is committed when we draw such a conclusion. To see this more clearly let us pause for a closer look at what we generally understand by the concept of 'cause.'

The concept of 'causation' is one of the most elusive in the history of thought. What is clear at the very outset, however, is that in order to rule out coincidence and establish causation, we must be able to say a lot more than that one event simply follows another.

For one thing, we must show that the sequence can be produced or interrupted at will under conditions that we specify in advance. Thus, if we wish to conclude that nitrogen mustard, an ointment, makes certain kinds of skin tumors shrink, we should be able to specify the method and frequency of application, and then repeatedly produce the desired tumor shrinkage under those conditions.

In this process we could of course feel some concern over whether it was the cream in which the mustard was based, or the massaging, or a placebo effect which caused the shrinkage. But proper experimental precautions together with our background knowledge generally enable us to control for, i.e., eliminate, many of these possibilities.

Having taken the above precautions, we may still be hesitant to say "cause." The two events involved may be more or less separated in space despite the fact that one succeeds the other in time, and this somehow violates our sense of intelligible causation. How can two events interact at a distance? Can they be causally linked unless there is "something" mediating between them; that is, unless they directly or indirectly "touch"? For example, how can we say that the sun pulls on the earth if they are separated by a huge vacuum?

In the case of the sun and the earth, theoretical physics provides the answer. It tells us that there is "something"—a gravitational field—that provides the needed connection across the 93 million miles that separate the sun from the earth. In the light of these considerations, it seems preposterous to believe that Columbus could have established a field of influence between himself and the celestial regions involved in the eclipse.

Even showing repeatability and space-time contiguity can leave us in need of more to really "nail down" a causal relation:

Not too long ago it was thought (and in some places still is) that breathing the foul air near swamps caused malaria. "Malaria," translated literally, means "bad air." In some southern European countries white poplars were grown alongside brooks where stagnant water might gather, not only as ornamentals and to hold top soil against flooding, but also because it was thought they would absorb the harmful air. No doubt people often *did* manifest the symptoms of malaria soon after visiting foul-smelling swampy regions. But, as we all know, it took considerable study, with the mighty microscope at center stage, to discover that inhaling foul air had nothing whatever to do with the burning fevers of malaria—being bitten by infected mosquitoes did.

We are all familiar with thunder and lightning and with the fact that we hear thunder a moment or two after the lightning has flashed. Actually, the more distant the lightning the greater the time interval between the two events. We can in fact roughly tell how far away the lightning is by noticing how long it takes to hear the thunder after seeing the lightning.*

Despite the lightning-thunder sequence meteorologists tell us that, rather than the lightning causing the thunder, both are caused by an electrical discharge. This releases energy which manifests itself mostly as heat. The heat violently expands the air to produce the clap of thunder and also causes the light which we see as a flash of lightning. This light travels enormously faster

---

*Simply take one-fifth of the time, in seconds, and the result is a rough estimate of the distance in miles.

than sound and therefore gets to us almost instantly in comparison to the later arrival of the sound.

Returning to our skin tumor example—it is known that nitrogen mustard attacks the DNA of body cells only during the process of cell division. Since tumor cells divide much more rapidly than normal cells the medication destroys mostly tumor cells with comparatively little effect on normal skin cells. Nitrogen mustard, therefore, can bring about (cause) a desirable effect on skin with tumors.

We can see by now that, at this advanced level of thinking, considerable scientific background can play into establishing a causal relation. Still, we sometimes know so little about some things that the best we can offer as grounds for claiming a causal relation is the fact that two events have occurred contiguously in both space and time. We might call this the case of primitive knowledge. In such a case, the argument for our claim is rather weak and we commit a fallacy if we offer it as a strong one. As we have seen, we strengthen our causal claim only after repeated instances of similar pairings. Our confidence reaches solid proportions as these instances become numerous and without exception. That very confidence is still further established when we can explain the sequence in terms of a successful model or theory describing the underlying mechanisms.

SYMPTOMS FOR CAUSES

We commit this fallacy when we choose one of two concurrent events as the cause (instead of effect or symptom) without having sufficient grounds for making the choice. Obviously, sufficient grounds for making this choice would require the kind of knowledge build-up we have just discussed in connection with simple succession. This, therefore, is a fallacy generally committed when such knowledge is incomplete.

For example, researchers have found aluminum in the brain tissue of people with Alzheimer's. This alone, however, would not be grounds for declaring aluminum to be a cause of the disease. The deposition of aluminum in brain tissue could, instead, be a symptom or side effect, rather than a cause. In such a case it could be either a direct metabolic consequence of the disease or there could be a third factor such as a pathogenic organism or a circulatory dysfunction which is causing both the disease and the aluminum deposits.

Distinguishing between symptoms and causes can be a very difficult matter. In the case of Alzheimer's, for example, medical scientists have *cautiously suggested* that a tough fibrous protein, beta-amyloid, found in the brain tissue of those suffering from the disease may be a causal factor. Very recently, however, one team of researchers has announced reasons for believing that beta-amyloid may instead be only a side effect rather than a cause of the disease. In this divergence of opinion, it is fair to say not that anyone has been reasoning fallaciously, but that the evidence has been insufficient to allow for any firm conclusion.

A symptoms-for-causes fallacy would have been committed if any conclusion had been submitted with more finality. Wary of this possibility, physicians often leave the more specific matter of causation open by saying of two concurrent events that they are "associated" rather than causally linked. Thus, beta-amyloid may quite safely still be said to be associated with Alzheimer's disease.

For another example imagine the following conversation between two friends at the office:

HARRY: You look like a spent cigar this morning. What's the matter, Bert?

BERT: I don't know, Harry, but for the past few days I haven't been sleeping well, and I've had frequent heart flutters.

HARRY: I remember once having a similar episode. I wasn't getting enough sleep and I was having a lot of heart flutters. Try to get more sleep, Bert. Some bedtime TV or a bit of cozying up with Meg can help you get to sleep sooner. That should take care of the heart flutters.

Harry is gratuitously concluding that insufficient sleep is causing Bert's arrhythmia. With some luck, he may be right—but he may also be dangerously wrong. Bert's insomnia may in fact be due to his heart problem rather than the other way around. The unwarranted conclusiveness with which Harry issues his recommendation makes his thinking fallacious and, in this case, possibly dangerous.

As a final example let me bring up the sort of thing one keeps hearing these days about attitude and health. The going popular wisdom seems to be that, after scrupulously defatting everything that goes into our mouths, the surest way to eternal health is a bright outlook on life. If, at a gathering of friends, you report that "Marc, whom we haven't seen for a long time, is as healthy and vigorous as ever," then, almost always, someone in the group will reply, "Well, Marc has a very positive, upbeat attitude about everything—doesn't he?" The implicit claim here is that Marc's positive attitude is one of the major factors contributing to his vigor and good health. Indeed, there seems to be some medical evidence for believing that optimistic attitudes can bolster the immune system. We also know, though, with at least as much certainty, that whenever we're feeling well we are more likely to be optimistic than when we're ailing. The authors of many of these remarks linking health to psychological causes may therefore be deciding fallaciously, i.e., on insufficient grounds, between symptom and cause.

REMOTE CAUSE: Got to Blame Someone or Something

This often cited jingle is worth repeating.

> For want of a nail a shoe was lost.
> For want of a shoe a horse was lost.
> For want of a horse a rider was lost.
> For want of a rider an army was lost.
> For want of an army a war was lost.
> For want of a victory a kingdom was lost.
> And all for the want of a nail.

Not quite! A kingdom was lost for want of a nail and, most likely, for want of many other things. The remote cause, here, is the circumstance that a horseshoe nail was unavailable when it was urgently needed, but clearly this did not have to be the only factor that toppled the kingdom. The authorities could have kept a reserve of nails or of well-shod horses. Or if not, they could have maintained some trained runners capable of running to some neighboring post where a rider might have been found. Or they could have kept still other forms of communication such as pigeons, drums, etc. The army involved might (possibly) have been strong enough and well-poised enough to have staved off defeat, after all. And, (possibly) the kingdom, itself, might not have fallen if it had been differently governed—even without the message that never got through "for want of a nail."

Haven't we all argued in the following crazy manner when we've had to blame someone?

LAURA: What on earth made me want dessert late last night?

TIM: Your damn whims, Laura, have cost us dearly. Did you really have to have that dessert last night? If it weren't for your insistence, we would not have driven three miles in the rain to find a restaurant, would not have gotten a flat and lost control of the car, and would not have crash landed in Jim Waterbagger's fish pond at two in the morning. Now we owe him $900 for damages. And we're lucky your sweet tooth didn't cost us our lives.

Tim is fanning the fires of guilt already burning in Laura's breast. He is, of course, ignoring the possibility of far more important contributing factors, such as bad tires or wipers, going too fast on wet pavement, bad driving skills, cataracts, night blindness, and possibly more. Any of these factors could have determined the course of events.

For cruder examples, we need only recall the countless cases of rape in which some commentaries have fallaciously shifted blame to the victim, pointing to attire, place, and time of day as "poor" choices which the victim made and without which the particular crime might not have occurred. Similarly, personal history and basic sociological conditions have been blamed as the causes of some crimes. The famous attorney Clarence Darrow is known to have won an acquittal for someone accused of murder by convincing a jury that it was society and not the defendant that was to be held causally responsible for the act. But given all that we know about how things happen and what we generally believe about the complexities of human decision making, action, and choice, it would be difficult to show, for some of these cases, that they did not involve at least *some* fallacious appeal to remote causes.

In need of a scapegoat or other bad guy "explanation," there is, of course, no limit to where one can go to find *the* cause of some event. The past offers us a limitless source of remote causes. How about blaming Tim's misfortune on Napoleon's aggression against England? It did lead to extreme financial pressure on France, which opened the way to the Louisiana Purchase, which made New Orleans American, which is where Tulane University was born, and which is where Laura, who came from Brooklyn forty years ago, studied nursing until she met Tim at a Mardi Gras party and settled down with him in New Orleans.

Appealing to something that is remote in time in order to explain some present state of affairs is, of course, not always fallacious. Exposure, many years ago, to asbestos, saron (a nerve gas), aniline dyes, or to some virus, may have a whole lot to do with someone's present condition. In such a case, what we know about the underlying biological mechanism assures us that the remote cause we are citing was probably a major player in bringing about the present condition. But when this sort of knowledge is missing, the appeal to remote causes is fallacious because it ignores the possibility—better still, the high likelihood—that other important factors have fed into the long chain of causes.

SINGLE CAUSE

> LAURA: Tim, I never wanted a sleep-in housekeeper who was young and you know it. Why on earth did you hire Odette?

> TIM: She came well-recommended and looked like the right one to me.

> LAURA: I'll bet she did. Tim, if you hadn't hired her, we would not have had that terrible brush fire.

> TIM: But how could I have known that a few days after she started, we would go to Sacramento for the weekend and that while we were there, her boyfriend would move in and throw lit cigarette butts around, eventually setting off the underbrush?

This no doubt has a familiar ring. We have to blame some one person or thing when we vent our anger, grief, or other stress by groping for a single cause of some unexpected and unwanted event. Here it is Laura who is jumping the gun. Obviously something is wrong with Laura's account of why it all happened. Tim seems to sense it but cannot quite put his finger on the error.

Apart from any personal motives on Tim's part in hiring a young housekeeper, the fact that he did so is at the very most one cause in a chain of causally connected events. But to call it the one, *single* cause of what happened is to commit the *single cause* fallacy—a fallacy closely related to the remote cause fallacy.

The events directly leading to the fire are a complex cluster of causal factors: Odette's character, which permitted her to break her promise not to entertain anyone without permission in the employer's house; her boyfriend's drinking habits, which led to intoxication and subsequent carelessness with his cigarette; months of drought, Tim's forgetting to hose and wet down the grass for the past ten days; poor clustering and positioning of the more inflammable bushes around the house; the strong Santa Anna winds; and no doubt more. Laura's attempt to pin it all on Tim's hiring of Odette is entirely unrealistic from any sort of explanatory point of view. She might not be doing much worse if she had blamed herself for having married Tim in the first place thirty years ago over her father's objections.

There is a second, more subtle defect in Laura's reasoning. In speaking of some relatively simple event like a billiard ball colliding with another one which is at rest or a gunman's bullet killing a pedestrian, there is no serious problem with speaking of *the* cause of the second billiard ball's sudden motion or of the pedestrian's death. In doing so, the points of view on the matter are about the same for all concerned and communication remains generally coherent and productive. Thus, hardly anyone would ever say that the second billiard ball's sudden lurch was due to the fact that it was lying there in the trajectory of the first ball, or that it was at rest rather than moving in the same direction as the first ball, or that the second billiard ball had a mass comparable to that of the first one, rather than one that was much larger. Nor is it likely that anyone would say that the wounded policeman's death was caused by his heart stopping or by the rise in his blood gas, or by his not wearing his bullet-proof vest.

When events are more complex, however, speaking of some factor as though it were the one and only cause can be greatly misguided and almost certainly unproductive. Laura blamed Tim for the fire, but Odette might have lamented, "that drunk boyfriend of mine." A nonsmoker might have muttered, "That barbaric smoking addiction." A meteorologist might have said, "Those bloody endless droughts we keep having in this part of California." And an extraterrestrial might have proclaimed, "That damn oxygen in this planet's atmosphere."

The "causes" that have been cited in this example happen to be the ones that interested the speakers. When the relativity to such interest is lost sight of, we fall into error. It is difficult to imagine, for example, just what sort of justification one could ever have for the single cause type of claim where complex human affairs are concerned. What single thing caused the breakup of the Soviet Union, the tragic rise of Hitler, or the past recession?

When a causal context is complex, we may still wish to conclude with a single, or perhaps better, *main* cause. This can depend on our purposes as, for example, what factors we can manipulate in a given situation. Unless the importance of this cause is obvious or properly shown, we risk arguing cross purposes in pointless disagreement.

SLIPPERY SLOPE: How Slippery?

The *slippery slope* fallacy is yet another muddle about causes, but we list it apart from the fallacies of false cause because of its special form, which makes it one of the handiest and most beguiling rhetorical weapons. It is used mostly by those who want to take a strong stand on a controversial issue, and it works by predicting an avalanche of events that will swish us down a "slippery slope" to some dreaded bottom. The fallacy is committed when this kind of doomsday prophesizing (often not very likely of fulfillment) is made without proper justification of all the problematic assumptions involved:

> National health insurance for every American? Why, that would cause medical costs to skyrocket! Everyone would be going to doctors. This would lead to inflation, which would in turn force a surge in interest rates, which would throttle the economy and lead to a recession, which would cause a reduction in government revenue, which in turn would swell the federal debt, which again would fuel inflation, resulting in still more upward pressure on interest rates, . . . and so on, 'til the collapse of the entire economy.

Even school economics tells us that this need not happen at all. Many other factors could impact on the chain of events and change its course. The government could exercise direct control on the prices of services, more frequent visits to the doctor could in fact serve to head off expensive operations, negotiations with the medical establishment to keep costs down might be more effective under more unified consumer group representation, and so on.

> If we allow government to tell us where we can or cannot smoke, all for our comfort and safety, we will soon be allowing it to tell us where we can or cannot drink, then where we can or cannot eat . . . ride, walk, talk, or live. We will by then have surrendered most of our liberties to Big Brother— all for our comfort and safety.

One famous appeal in favor of our entering the Vietnam conflict was the so-called domino effect:

> If all of Vietnam goes communist, so will the rest of Indochina, and, as a result, India and the rest of free Asia. Finally, the rest of the world will follow.

That a chain of this sort was at all probable called for proper justification, and when this wasn't done a slippery slope was committed. The fact that this slippery slope pronouncement actually turned out to be false dramatizes the importance of providing ample grounds for sweeping claims of this sort.

Remember this one?

> If I hatch the eggs in this basket instead of eating them, I can raise the chicks for a while and then sell them. With the proceeds I will buy a pair of baby pigs, mate them, and so on, until I buy an entire farm.

Again, as the famous fable teaches us, the fallacy here consists of failing to recognize that the causal chain can be broken at any link by the highly probable intrusion of other causal factors. The eggs may not all hatch, the chickens may not all survive or sell, and so on.

DIVISION: Dividing without Conquering

The fallacy of *division* stems from a subtle conceptual confusion, and the victim is often as much the author as the audience. Still, when it is committed it can be very disorienting.

For a start, let us go to some examples:

A few years ago, a wealthy socialite defending herself against serious income tax charges declared that she had paid millions in taxes that year. This would certainly be a lot of money, but did the amount she paid cover each portion of her income, or were there portions of income that she illegally shielded from taxation? Conceivably, because of some accounting error, she could have even paid more than the law required. Even so, her tax return would still be fraudulent if she deliberately failed to report some portion of her income.

> Enough on teachers' raises. They're being paid amply. The combined outlay for teachers' salaries throughout this state goes into the billions.

In this example, the total outlay for teachers' salaries may be large. This, however, does not guarantee that each salary, i.e., each part of that outlay, is adequate compensation for the individual teacher.

Arguments of this sort are rampant, though their fallaciousness is usually pretty obvious. The examples show that if a whole possesses a certain property the part may or may not possess it. So, unless we have good reasons to the contrary, any inference in which we carry some property from the whole to the part can have a false or even ludicrous conclusion.

> Rhinoceroses are gradually disappearing. Therefore, the rhino in our zoo is gradually disappearing.

> Men who carry handbags are now seen on the streets of every country in Europe. My uncle is a man who carries a handbag.

Therefore he is now seen on the streets of every country in Europe.

The Germans are wealthier than the Rumanians. Therefore, our German neighbor, Hans Kimmel, is wealthier than our Rumanian neighbor, Nino Zane.

The cake is spongy. Therefore, the ingredients in the cake are spongy.

Let us pause here for an historically important consideration involving the fallacy of division. Following the lead of the great seventeenth-century French philosopher and mathematician René Descartes, our intellectual orientation for the past three centuries has been strongly analytical. Roughly speaking, this is a method of thought in which we attempt to understand a complex whole by breaking it down into its elemental parts and then examining the properties of these simpler elements. Having done this we can hopefully gain some basic knowledge about the original whole.

The analytic method is not to be sold short. It has certainly had a glorious history of success, especially in science, where it still holds center stage. Some authors, however, have expressed serious objections to it, claiming that the fallacy of division is inherent in it.

The danger of fallacy however lies not in the use of analysis but in its misuse. In dividing a whole into elemental parts, we must not fail to think in terms of relations. The properties of any element—its color, its taste, its attractiveness, whether or not it is alive, etc.—may themselves depend on how the element relates in fundamental ways to the whole. The analysis must, in this sense, be holistic. The possibility of any such dependency must be allowed for, or the analysis is incomplete and therefore seriously flawed.

Simple examples of improper analysis are easily given but are not very instructive because their incorrectness is obvious and easily avoided. If, for example, we say of a live individual that she consists of (may be analyzed as) a number of live parts—hands, arms, feet, etc.—we of course understand that these parts are alive only if they remain properly attached to the body. Once detached, they die and remain dead. Similarly, if we characterize a given marriage by saying that it consists of two miserable people, we of course may have to keep in mind and consider the possibility that these two people may be miserable only in the relationship. Apart they may be very much okay and even joyful of life.

Here's a really imaginary but more instructive example involving a weird, hypothetical kind of construction material:

Imagine a masonry manufacturer who makes a most remarkable brick—one whose color changes with the pressure on it. At ordinary pressures the brick is grey. At somewhat higher pressures it begins to turn brown. As the pressure increases beyond this, the brick turns more and more red. A wall made with bricks of this sort will be red at the bottom, less red and more brown near the middle, less brown and more grey further up, and grey at the top. A characterization (analysis) that we might give of the wall by saying that it consists of bricks that vary from grey at the top to red at the bottom will be incomplete and seriously misleading.

A more appropriate analysis would characterize the wall as consisting of bricks whose color is grey when the brick is detached from the wall and anything from grey to red when the brick is part of the wall depending on how low down the brick is placed during construction. This leaves open the possibility— remote though it may be—that the color the brick exhibits depends on how much compression the brick is under. This of course, is a purely hypothetical example. In any actual context even a layman would know that the bricks in the wall are not likely to be of a sort that change color under pressure.

There is, of course, a fundamental difficulty in any attempt to give a useful relational analysis. For any given whole or totality, there is no limit to the number of possible relations between it and its parts. If so, then how do we decide which are the relevant relations for inclusion in the analysis?

In general, this is a more or less complex matter of background knowledge, trained judgment, purpose, and so on. Strictly speaking, therefore, we never know with absolute certainty that any attempt to analyze a whole into its elements has taken into account every relevant relationship. We commit the fallacy of division, however, when, in attempting any analysis, we simplistically overlook the possibility of having to consider the relevant relationships.

Now for a very common and dangerous but rarely discussed form of the fallacy of division: the *the-less-the-better* version. We commit this fallacy as soon as we reason that reducing the amount of anything automatically reduces its effects. For example, one might want to argue the following points:

- Stress is bad. Therefore less stress is better and no stress at all is best.
- Ten grams of zinc are harmful. Therefore one gram is less harmful, and no zinc at all is best.
- Aerobic exercise three times a week is good for you. Therefore the same exercise once a month is not as good but better than none.
- Dietary fat is bad. Therefore no fat at all is best.

But medical scientists tell us that

- Some stress is better than no stress at all—even if a zero-stress existence were possible.
- No zinc at all could lead to illness; indeed, ten to fifteen milligrams of zinc is a minimum daily requirement for practically all adults.
- There is reason to believe that infrequent aerobic exercise may, in fact, be harmful.
- Some dietary fat is necessary for the absorption of certain vitamins.

Those who commit the the-less-the-better fallacy are very likely not trying to put anything over on anyone. They, themselves, as much as the ones they are trying to help, are usually unwary victims. In many cases as we reduce the quantity of something, we in fact also reduce its effects—sometimes even proportionately so. For example, the weight of any substance is directly related to the amount of it (its mass), as is toxicity in the case of many poisons. To avoid the fallacy one must provide additional premises containing evidence that the the-less-the-better relationships which are being assumed do, in fact, hold. Reasoning without such grounds is fallacious and can have ruinous consequences.

COMPOSITION: Don't Dare Bet on It!

The fallacy of *composition* is the "inverse" of the fallacy of division and is committed when we uncritically attribute to the whole some property of the part.

An example:

> When it was his turn to speak at a meeting of a large, financially troubled corporation, a section head, possibly hoping to shield his particular department from blame of inefficiency, cautiously slipped in the claim that each one of his people had been hired according to the highest company standards and was superbly qualified to do his job.

We must be careful in unveiling the fallacy this section head may have been committing. If all he was attempting to do was to point out that for a department to function properly it is a necessary condition that its members each be competent, then his reasoning is pretty much okay. But, instead, he may be attempting to argue that the competence of each staff member is a sufficient condition for overall efficiency, or, putting it differently, that from the premise that each member is a good worker one can conclude that the department will be a good one. If this is the point of his comment, then he is reasoning fallaciously. Quite obviously, it takes much more than the excellence of each employee (the part) to make an excellent department (the whole). The department, for one thing, must be organized in a way that makes it possible for the employees to utilize their capacities and to interact with each other productively.

The following arguments are more obviously fallacious:

Every tile Antonio uses in his mosaics is beautiful. No wonder his mosaics are so beautiful.

Hydrogen and oxygen, under normal conditions, are highly incendiary. Therefore water, which is composed of these two substances, is highly incendiary.

And here is an interesting (paraphrased) example attributed to the ancient philosopher Zeno of Elea:

Consider any two places, say New York and Chicago. In order for me to go from New York to Chicago, I must first get to the mid-point between them. But once I get to this mid-point, I still cannot reach Chicago unless I first get to the mid-point of the remaining distance. And so on. There will, it seems, always be a distance between Chicago and me whose midpoint I have not yet reached. Therefore I can never quite reach Chicago.

This argument can be extended further to yield an even more astounding conclusion:

Before I reach the first mid-point, I must reach an earlier mid-point, namely, the mid-point of the distance between myself and that first mid-point. But before I reach that second mid-point, I must first reach a still earlier mid-point, namely, the midpoint of the distance between myself and the second mid-point. It appears, therefore, that there will always be an earlier mid-point closer and closer to me that I have yet to reach. And so, it seems I can never even leave New York. And since in place of New York I could have considered any starting point whatever, it seems that motion of any sort is impossible.

Ancient and distinguished though the source of this reasoning may be, it quite definitely smacks of fallacy. For though
it rests on what seem to be impeccable premises, the conclusion
is patently false. In general, I have no trouble whatever traversing the entire distance from New York to Chicago and can
even go on to a third city if I so choose.

Despite the very suspicious character of the reasoning it is no
easy matter to say precisely where the argument goes wrong. The
reasoning takes us from parts (the trip segments) to a whole (the
full trip). Now, the parts are infinite in number and therefore
impossible to traverse entirely (as would be impossible to count
them all), one at a time. On this basis, Zeno concludes that the
whole is also impossible to encompass fully.

Unfortunately, the considerations here are complex and elusive enough to have taken philosophers and mathematicians two
thousand years to get a handle them. A responsible discussion of
Zeno's Paradox, as this argument is called, would take us quite
beyond our purposes here into some of the concepts of higher
mathematics. It is enough to point out that though there is,
indeed, always an untraversed distance segment confronting me
as I move from New York to Chicago, something else is also
true. Each of the intervening segments gets smaller and smaller
as I get closer and closer to B. Each is half as large as the one
before. Traversing the entire distance, therefore, means traversing a sequence of rapidly diminishing segments. We can
therefore imagine the possibility that though there are an infinite
number of such segments, I can nevertheless add them up to
yield a definite, i.e., finite, quantity, namely the distance from
New York to Chicago. (The methods for successfully adding up
infinite sequences of ever-diminishing terms is a matter for that
branch of mathematics known as the infinitesimal calculus.) On
the level of concrete practical action, we can interpret the idea of
totaling up our infinite number of gradually vanishing segments
of the trip as nothing other than my physically traversing the
total distance of the trip.

Very broadly speaking, Zeno's argument is fallacious in that its conclusion does not follow from its premises. The argument overlooks the fact that an infinite number of parts *can* add up to a finite whole. Indeed it is no great stretch of the imagination for me to think of any ordinary (finite) object as something which I can divide unendingly into smaller and smaller parts. The number of such parts will increase without limit while the size of the particles diminishes toward the vanishing point. My perfectly finite whole therefore can be thought of as the "summation" of an unending or "infinite" number of vanishing parts.

Let us go now to a time-honored example of the fallacy of composition, the color spectrum paradox. As in the case of Zeno's Paradox, its importance is more theoretical than practical, but it is nevertheless interesting.

> If we go from red to orange on a spectrum of colors we can move in steps that are small enough so that we cannot detect any color difference between our first red and our second, between our second and our third, and so on through a large number of successively undetectable differences until we get to orange. There is therefore no real detectable color difference between red and orange.

This obviously fallacious argument takes us uncritically from a property of the component steps in a process (imperceptibility of change at each part of the process) to a presumed property of the whole product (imperceptibility of change for the entire process).

Finally, and only for symmetry and completeness, we should mention a version of the fallacy of composition that we might label the *the-more-the-better* fallacy. You'll note, it is quite obviously the inverse of the the-less-the-better fallacy discussed under the fallacy of division. The points to be made about this fallacy are essentially the same as those we made about the the-less-the-better fallacy. And so, to avoid repeating we will simply look at two examples. The flawed thinking in them will be obvious in the light of our earlier discussion:

It is fairly well established that one very small aspirin tablet (81 milligrams) per day helps reduce the risk of heart attack in certain groups. So, why not simply take a regular aspirin tablet which is about four times as large (320 milligrams)? Shouldn't it give even more—perhaps four times the—protection?

Vitamin C seems to be effective in fighting off, and perhaps forestalling, the common cold. So let's take megadoses of vitamin C and banish the bane of human existence.

As a matter of fact, medical scientists tell us that more than 81 milligrams of aspirin daily can affect the arteries adversely, thus neutralizing the anticoagulant benefits derivable from the much smaller dose. Similarly, we are warned that megadoses of vitamin C can have adverse side effects such as crystallization ("stone" formation) in the kidneys.

Like the the-less-the-better fallacy, the the-more-the-better fallacy is a very dangerous one which is frequently committed largely because in many cases the effects of things do in fact increase as we increase their quantity. But in this regard, we easily recall that though one pinch of salt may be good for the sauce, twenty pinches will not make it food for Queen Hatshepsut.

Obviously, this form of the fallacy of composition is the dangerous case of "a little knowledge" and a lot of oversimplification which can victimize both the author and any others he advises. To escape the fallacy the author must, in his premises, present evidence supporting the assumption that increasing the dosage will increase the benefit.

※　※　※

In our next chapter, we take up the last three of our twenty standard fallacies. I have left these for last because they're subtle and therefore very difficult to respond to. What is more, their subtlety easily hides their fallaciousness, and this makes them especially insidious in their rhetorical force and ability to convince.

12

ELUSIVE TRICKERY:
Watch Out!

SELF-INTEREST: Only Half the Story

More than any other, the fallacy of *self-interest* can stop you dead in your tracks. It not only puts one on the defensive; it takes careful reflection to expose its flaw. Overall, this fallacy is probably even more disarming than question begging, whose deceptive and elusive subtleties were discussed in chapter 7.

We commit the fallacy of self-interest when we argue, cynically, that there is no such thing as altruism because whenever one acts on someone's behalf she does so only to please herself. So—as the reasoning goes—in final analysis even the actions we standardly call "altruistic" are no less selfish than those we standardly call "selfish." We have here an argument which, in effect, obliterates the long-standing "common sense" distinction between selfish and unselfish acts. And this alone should rouse our suspicions about its merits.

An example:

BERT: Your sister, who is much busier than you, visits your aging mother weekly. I'm surprised you're not contributing some visits of your own. I have generally thought you to be the considerate one. But in fact she is the one who is carrying the ball.

HARRY: Bert, my sister is making no sacrifice by going to see my mother.

BERT: How so, Harry?

HARRY: Quite simple, Bert. She goes because she wants to; and because doing what she wants to do, as in the case of anyone else, is what gives her pleasure. Her only purpose, therefore, is to pursue her own ends, her own pleasure. So, you see, she is no more altruistic than I am. Like the rest of us, she desires nothing other than her own satisfactions, and she gets these by visiting our mother. I, instead, do not enjoy going there and get my kicks doing other things.

Harry's reply, of course, easily raises serious doubts, for it fails to distinguish two modes of conduct that differ in a morally relevant way. Harry's conduct is indifferent to his mother's welfare. His sister's, on the other hand, seems more benevolent or—as we say—more altruistic. None of us, I'm sure, would be inclined to regard the two kinds of conduct as morally equivalent.

Well then, where has Harry's reasoning gone wrong? The trouble, as in any fallacy, is that he draws a conclusion which does not follow from his premises. To see this, let us grant him that his sister *does* want to see her mother and that doing so *does* give her great pleasure. From this, however, it does not follow, despite Harry's confident conclusion, that all she is after with her visits is her own pleasure.

Arguments like Harry's are especially objectionable when they are generalized. The grandiose idea is that all we're ever after in our actions is our own pleasure; that all we ever do or say is ultimately self-serving.

True, when we accomplish what we want to accomplish we usually feel good. We feel a sense of fulfillment and well-being —yes, pleasure, if you like. But the conclusion that therefore such pleasure is always our sole and deliberate aim in doing what we want to do does not follow at all. It is like concluding that because joggers put more wear on their sneakers whenever they jog, the purpose of their jogging is to wear out their sneakers— possibly, even to enjoy the experience of acquiring new ones.

I generally enjoy a clean shave. Sometimes I have no other reason for shaving. This hardly justifies concluding that, in general, I shave only for the sheer pleasure of shaving. I may shave primarily to look clean-shaven or simply to please others. Similarly, Harry's sister may derive pleasure—even great pleasure— before, during, and after visiting her aging mother, but it is fallacious for Harry to conclude from this that his sister must be acting from no other motive. She could be doing it to give her mother pleasure, to bolster her mother's morale, or simply because it seems to be the right thing to do.

THE CONSEQUENCES OF BELIEVING:
Can We Believe on Purpose?

How convincing do you find the following arguments?

> We must all believe in God or else face increasing violence, crime, and irresponsibility.

> Don't be a fatalist. It will rob you of all ambition and you will never accomplish anything.

> Stop believing the streets are unsafe and you will start enjoying your evening walks downtown.

> If you don't stop doubting that your lover is true, you will despair to the breaking point.

> We had better believe that our side is right if we are to win this war.

Let us offer that senator a hefty contribution to his election campaign. That ought to help him believe that our new bomber merits a military contract.

A familiar evangelical message:

Believe in God and you will be healed.

A no less historical figure than the great seventeenth-century French scientist and mystic, Blaise Pascal, gave something like the following argument for believing in God:

I take less risk if I believe that God exists than if I do not. For if I do so believe and he exists then I will not be punished for my disbelief. If, on the other hand, he does not exist, I lose nothing.

In all these arguments the authors recommend or urge that we believe something simply because a desirable consequence would result from the act of doing so. Although some of the arguments may at first seem appealing, we easily sense that there is something seriously wrong with all of them, no matter how high the authority of their sources. Unfortunately, however, when we try to say exactly how they go wrong, the going gets very difficult. Indeed, this fallacy seems to be the hardest of all to debunk.

To help pinpoint the problem, consider for a moment an argument which is superficially similar to our first example, yet differs from it in one very important respect:

We must provide our youth with job-training and job opportunities or else face increasing violence, crime, and irresponsibility.

Unlike our first example, which recommends that we all believe in God in order to avoid increasing violence, crime, and irresponsibility, this argument recommends providing something instead of believing something in order to bring about the desired result. In so doing it raises no difficulty of the sort we sense with our first example. The trouble seems to be the concept of "believing." We can always act to provide job and job-training opportunities in order to reduce street crime, but can we simply start believing in God in order to achieve the same result?

This is not to say that believing might not work—it may indeed be true that once we believe in God we will have less street crime. (Whether or not this is in fact so can be decided only on the basis of sociological inquiry.) The trouble, however, is that believing in anything seems to call for more than just a recommendation.

Believing in God means believing there is in fact a God, which in turn means believing the claim "God exists" is true or at least probable. But the consequences (benefits) to be reaped from holding this belief have no bearing whatever on its truth. To establish support for believing in God, we might have to ponder the "miracle" of consciousness, the cosmological order, the problem of good and evil, the need for justice, or some other philosophical issues whose answers could conceivably count for or against the belief. But the claim that having the belief would improve our conduct would certainly not be a truth-supporting reason for the belief. The argument in this first example and those in our other examples are therefore fallacious. The fallacy in them is standardly known as the consequences of believing fallacy.

OUR DEEPLY EPISTEMIC NATURE

Quite apart from its illogic, this fallacy is to some extent "naturally" or, as we might say, psychologically, unavailing. In actual practice, we ordinarily demure when simply asked to believe on irrelevant grounds. A belief is not generally something I can adopt at will because doing so will make me more comfortable, healthy, prosperous, nonviolent, loving, or blessed in any way. I simply cannot convince myself that I am independently wealthy on the basis of the comfort and sense of economic power that such a belief (if I held it) would give me. To be convinced, I would have to consider my actual assets, liabilities, liquidity, and so on.

Were some of us to believe that commercial flying is entirely safe, we would, as a consequence, certainly enjoy air travel more. But this consequence has nothing to do with the actual safety of air travel and therefore with the truth or falsity of our beliefs about it. We all know this. We know what the factors relevant to safety are. They are not the comfort or discomfort that our beliefs about air safety may produce. They are, instead, factors like the age and condition of the aircraft in service, the quality of crews and maintenance, the extent of security, the weather patterns and geography along air routes, and perhaps most of all, the safety records of the carriers in the industry. These, therefore, are the matters which will naturally go into establishing our confidence in flying and not any appeal to the enjoyment that might result from that confidence.

Most cosmologists today are convinced that, probably, the universe is finite rather than infinite in size. But this belief stems not from its being the "cozier" one (infinity in this case seems to be more scary). It stems from the fact that a finite universe best accounts for what astronomers are discovering with their telescopes.

I have at last come to believe that if I leave the saucepan on a hot plate, I run the risk of forgetting it there and converting its contents to smoke and ashes. This now firm conviction puts me in better harmony, at least as far as kitchen matters are concerned, with my wife, who never tires of reminding me of the risk. But the happy consequence of cordial kitchen dynamics is not what has fixed my conviction. Rather, it is the fact that I have countless times forgotten the saucepan on the burner and charred its contents.

Another way of putting all this is to say that yes, we are to a considerable extent rational in the way we fix our beliefs, however irrational we may be in all our other stances. Our epistemic hunger is virtually insatiable. We're not cats, but our curiosity often knows no bounds as we try to build our convictions— sometimes almost recklessly—on relevant evidence rather on the emotional effects or other consequences of the convictions. We do this even when the news is from the pathologist, the site of the air disaster, or the battlefront. We are, for the most part, incurable "suckers" for "the truth."

Belief, then, is what we might call a *cognitive* or *knowledge-related* attitude, more technically, an epistemic orientation. (The Greek word for knowledge is *episteme*.) It is a truth-related orientation that we acquire in the context of evidence.

But not always. It would be futile to deny that we also have some tendency to believe something if we want to believe it strongly enough. This "counter-rational" tendency manifests itself most dramatically when anxiety creates a craving for self-deception. Most of us know how, under stress, we can "psyche" ourselves into believing the most unlikely claims. In the extreme, self-deception can even shade into loss of contact with reality and psychotic dysfunction.

And what about those unjustified widespread beliefs, pro or con some human group? Aren't chauvinism and bigotry sometimes cultivated for their political and emotional perks despite the fact that such lapses of rationality can be wide of the mark and even pose a social menace?

In cases of this sort, where belief seems nourished by personal stakes, the act of acceptance seems not to be a truly voluntary one. I would say that it is, rather, a reactive state produced by duress, and often where there is substantial uncertainty as to what in fact is or is not true. If so, then recommending that we adopt this or that belief on the basis of its consequences can be seen as having no purpose other than to soften the listener's critical faculties so as to pave the way for some unjustified belief. Does this mean that we should shun anything smacking of the consequences of belief fallacy?

HOPES AND IDEALS

By now, you will surely want to say that there are cases in which believing something is so beneficial either personally or socially that we ought, somehow, to get ourselves to that state of conviction and perhaps even cultivate it, despite all the unfavorable evidence. (Again, our natural resistance to believing without truth-supports presents the same daunting difficulties.) To say we ought to implies we can and, this, as we have seen, is no simple, voluntary sense of "can."

Still we do, it seems, manage somehow to achieve and even cherish certain "desirable" orientations—attitudes, if you like—largely because it feels good or, in some sense, is appropriate to do so. "Believing" that one's country is right, that a loved one is innocent, that political solutions are better than military ones, or that benevolent reciprocity is better than inter-reactive hostility is "believing" of this kind. The consequences recommend such "believing" even in the absence of tangible truth-related evidence.

Given what we have seen to be the knowledge-related or epistemic nature of belief, however, it seems to make more sense to regard desirable, positive orientations less as beliefs and more as hopes, or ideals for the guidance of action, or simply as deeply felt wishes. The term "belief-like attitudes" would perhaps be best here.

Be this as it may, such optative states of mind (those characterized by desire or choice) are sometimes all that preserve our sanity and keep us going in the face of odds that can be dismal enough to crush even the most spirited. In such cases recommending that one be hopeful or loyal or generally "positive" for the sake of consequences would not be fallacious. It would merely be an opener for cultivating useful attitudes known to promote our survival.

MADNESS

Ought we to ever drop our guard against madness? In the gloom of despair or under the pressure of fear, we can slide from hopeful thinking to utter self-deception. Ideologies can become cults and hope can shade into delusion. In Arthur Miller's play *All My Sons,* Kate's firm belief that her son, a World War II pilot, is still alive may well be what keeps her from cracking altogether. But as the time passes and the unfavorable evidence mounts, her unswerving belief becomes a serious reality distortion that threatens to take her to the brink of madness.

What seems important to note in all this is that belief-like attitudes are most easily acquired in the context of uncertainty, when the truth of what we "try" to believe is largely unsettled. In such a case, being urged to "think positive," even when the chances are against us, may be understood not as a request to change our beliefs but rather as a recommendation to focus attention on the more favorable possibilities, slim though these may be.

In doing this we need not—and ordinarily cannot—make ourselves believe likely what we know to be unlikely. We can, however, envision, entertain, or otherwise keep in mind the more favorable possibilities without loss of reality contact. It is enough to know that the likelihood of the favorable possibility is significant, though perhaps much less than its unlikelihood. And since we have in all this no request to change or adopt any belief but only a recommendation to contemplate and focus on—i.e., to hope for—the favorable possibility, the consequences-of-believing fallacy is not involved. Such a recommendation therefore need pose neither a logical nor a psychological impasse for those who cannot believe except on good grounds.

Before closing on this puzzling fallacy, let us consider briefly a very special kind of "consequences" recommendation which escapes the fallacy we have been discussing even more decisively than does simply recommending hopeful thinking. Recall that a hopeful, positive outlook is, on standard medical opinion, an important therapeutic factor in the treatment of human illness, or that self-confidence can help achieve our goals, or that what people believe about the economy can have a strong effect on how it will in fact go. These are what social scientists call self-fulfilling prophesies (hopes, beliefs)—factors which they take seriously in their projections.

BELIEVING CAN HELP MAKE IT SO

Clearly, we cannot dismiss off-hand the possibility that what we focus on and hope for in certain contexts will affect what we end up getting. Indeed, students of the subject no longer hesitate to tell us that recommending positive or hopeful attitudes is decidedly not fallacious, not only on the basis of the considerations we've made so far but also because, in fact, what we hope for, contemplate, focus on, and even believe, can, to some extent "make it happen." In this sense the consequences of our belief-like attitudes are directly relevant to the truth of what we are hoping, focusing on, or wanting to believe. In such a case, recommending a positive attitude is decidedly free of fallacious overtones. And though "thinking" (imagining) something to be so may not simply and assuredly make it so, it sometimes can—especially where human aspiration is involved—help make it so.

THE PSYCHOLOGISTIC FALLACY:
Does Explaining Actions Justify Them?

We have seen in chapter 2 that to justify (support) a claim we must give reasons for believing it to be true. We can then go on to an explanation (as detailed in chapter 4) by citing the causes of what the claim reports. And as we have also noted, the explanation is also supportive of the truth of the claim to which we fit it.

Justifying an action (not a claim) is, however, a very different matter. To justify an action, we must establish the grounds for believing it to be (morally) right, ultimately by appealing to moral principles. This separates moral justification radically from explanation.

The explanation of an act gives us its psychodynamics, i.e., the psychological "forces," emotions, habits, purposes, attitudes, and so on, that drove someone (the agent) to commit the act. The daunting question then is, Does such an explanation justify the act? In general, the answer to this question is, as we shall see, no, and when we offer an explanation as a moral justification, we therefore commit the *psychologistic fallacy.*

Before going further with this rather tricky matter, let us consider a concrete example to help fix our ideas. Here is my reconstruction of something I heard recently at a gathering of experts on foreign policy:

> A: How can we justify the embargo we have imposed on Cuba over the past thirty years?
>
> B: Well, we've done it because we have feared Cuba's policy of exporting Marxist revolutions.
>
> A: Yes, but ought we to have imposed such crushing economic hardship on the people of our tiny neighbor?
>
> B: Well this has been a method, short of war, of forcing the Cuban government to change its ways. As you know, we did try war at the Bay of Pigs, and look what happened.
>
> A: Yes, but . . .

A and B in this conversation are verging on a very common sort of muddle. They are talking at cross-purposes. Or, perhaps better, they are having two conversations at once. A is looking to find a moral justification for our Cuban policy. B wants to explain it in terms of our desire to change Cuba's ways. If, as B is claiming, our aim in imposing sanctions has been to force Cuba to change its ways, then in order to establish the rightness of our policy she would have to say something about the rightness of this aim, and this B has not done. As a justification of our Cuban policy, therefore, B's argument is fallacious.

DOES EXPLANATION EVER JUSTIFY ACTIONS?

True, the rightness of an action is ordinarily established by "measuring" it and the motives behind it against the moral principles or ethics by which we live, rather than by explaining it in terms of the drives that move it. Here we encounter a serious problem, however. In holding anyone morally responsible we implicitly assume that he can freely choose to act either ethically or unethically despite the motives or other emotional forces that can drive the action. On such an assumption, citing the causes of an action, though useful in explaining it, would be irrelevant to its moral justification.

The ever-haunting question, however, is, Just how free are we to choose our actions? Our marked tendency to offer explanations as moral justifications may well stem from the persistent doubts we have about how to answer this question.

INCONTINENCE: The Moral Force of Explanations

The assumption that an agent (one who acts) is in fact free to choose, is not only a matter of age-old and deep philosophical controversy, but it also frequently becomes a concrete issue on very practical levels. Given all the "forces" that move the agent, how evident is it that she is free to do otherwise? And if so, in what precise sense of 'free'? It would not be profitable here to ponder this issue, usually referred to as the problem of "free will"—surely one of the most difficult and controversial in the entire history of philosophy.

For our purposes, however, it is enough to note that in extreme cases we do in fact allow explanations to count, to some extent, as exonerations if not as justifications. We do this when the agent is so driven by pain, fear, or other stresses as to cast serious doubt on just how "free" he is to choose to do otherwise. We can easily identify cases in which the agent is hardly free at all: intoxication, addiction, terror, torture, panic, psychoses, etc. Any of these could, it seems, largely deprive him of his moral autonomy and render him "beside himself."

The ancient philosopher Aristotle, more than two thousand years ago, used the term "incontinent" to describe anyone in such a state, the idea being that such an individual cannot be held entirely responsible for what he does. Largely driven by forces beyond his control, he is in such a case essentially robot-like and no more autonomous than a billiard ball buffeted by the impacting forces that compel its motion. The totally incontinent individual does not deliberate, make free decisions, or engage in genuine conduct. Rather than acting, he merely behaves. Consequently, the context of such behavior is no longer a moral one and we can therefore neither approve of nor condemn it. We can only explain it much as we explain the predatory activities of lions or the necessary motions of the planets.

Nowadays we also make allowances for moral "incontinence." When circumstances are too compelling for a reasonable person to withstand, we make allowances for an action that we would ordinarily condemn. Even when the forces driving a person are not entirely overwhelming we usually temper our disapproval. We see the forces under which he has acted as morally "mitigating" to the extent that they distorted his judgment.

LEGAL MITIGATION

This sort of allowance is, as we all know, also made in law where an explanation in terms of the force of circumstances can sometimes reduce the severity of a verdict. Recall, for example, how an act is sometimes described as a "crime of passion" or, in more extreme cases, as something done under either temporary or chronic insanity or under extreme duress imposed by some threatening party or circumstance. In every civilized society the law distinguishes between a crime committed under compelling emotional forces and one committed "in cold blood."

It is this possibility of appealing to mitigating or extenuating circumstances that makes it tempting to explain an action even when the circumstances are really *not* so mitigating or extenuating. And this, together with the inherent subtleties in the issue, no doubt largely accounts for the tendency to confuse the explanation of an act with its moral justification.

Despite the possible moral relevance of the causes that move an action, it is important, even urgent, to distinguish explaining the act from morally justifying it. Blurring explanation with moral justification not only compromises our understanding and critical thinking, it easily leads to wasteful disputation at cross-purposes. The resulting confusion can seriously hamper communication and even raise frustration levels to the point of hostility, thus seriously jeopardizing the chances of harmonious and fruitful discourse.

Pundits at colloquiums are not the only ones who confuse explanation with moral justification. Here is a version of something I heard not too long ago on a popular television show.

A: Wasn't it monstrous of those Serbian soldiers to shoot up a truckful of captured civilian villagers, mostly women and children?

B: Well, what else can you expect? There have been atrocities like that on both sides of this conflict and by now there is nothing but anger and hate. The groups involved have lived together in mutual abhorrence for centuries, and they're not about to stop now.

A: But isn't it still wrong for them to kill that way—slaughtering helpless innocents—no matter how angry or hateful they feel while they're doing it?

B: I wonder how you would feel, sir, if some people did that to your whole family. Wouldn't you want to do the same thing to them?

＊　　＊　　＊

Back in part one of our discussion, we viewed the general anatomy of *good* arguments, while in part two, we have just examined the most common kinds of *bad* arguments. But what we've done so far leaves as a total mystery the most fundamental question of all, indeed of all logic, namely, What makes reasoning so compelling? What marvelous relationship is there between premises and conclusion that gives an argument its uniquely irresistible thrust?

To get some hold on the answer, let's begin part three of our voyage. There, we can navigate a bit closer to land for an arm's-reach look at the two basic forms of all reasoning: deductive and nondeductive (inductive) reasoning.

Part Three

THE TWO LOGICAL FORMS:
Deductive and Inductive

13

THE FABULOUS LOGIC:
An Age-Old Myth

THE OLD FAVORITE: Deduction

We once had a very intelligent shepherd dog who had for a time used one or the other of our two stairways to the boys' bedroom. On one occasion, as a crude experiment, I suddenly placed an obstacle in her path just as she started up one of the stairways. She stopped for a split moment, reversed her course, bounded across two rooms to the other stairway—and up she went.

Bertrand Russell is known to have said: "If dogs can think, why don't they say so?" Samba (that was her name) actually said nothing. But her thinking could have been

> Hm-m-m, either this one or the other one.
> Not this one.
> Therefore
> The other one.

And it would have been a neat bit of deductive reasoning. Logicians have a name for it: the *disjunctive syllogism.*

Deduction has been traditionally regarded as the ideal form of reasoning. It certainly holds center stage in mathematics and plays a crucial role in the basic quantitative sciences. As a result, the writings in logic have been mostly about deductive reasoning.

Our own discussion departs from this tradition, simply because reasoning of a kind other than deductive plays the greater role. Nevertheless, a brief encounter with it will afford us some basic logical concepts together with a few key reasoning strategies. So we'll take a passing look at it.

Consider the following very simple examples of deduction:

> If Bob is wise, he'll be cautious. But, Bob is wise. Therefore, he will be cautious.

> Either Socrates wanted fame or he wanted justice. Fame he did not want. Therefore, he wanted justice.

> If the evidence had been conclusive, then the court would have convicted her. The court did not convict her. Therefore, the evidence was not conclusive.

> Jupiter is larger than Earth and Earth is larger than Mars. Therefore, Jupiter is larger than Mars.

> All guppies are born alive. My fish are all guppies. Therefore, they were all born alive.

Here is one that is a bit less simple:

> If Priscilla is dutiful, she will marry Miles. If she is wise she will marry John. But either Priscilla is dutiful or she is wise. Therefore, she will either marry Miles or she will marry John.

Most of these are instances of simple argument forms to which logicians have given fancy Latin names that we will not bother with here. In formal reasoning, these standard mini-forms serve as building-blocks for constructing long and sometimes complex proofs.

DEDUCTIVE VALIDITY

On almost immediate inspection it becomes obvious that, in each of the above examples, the premises give the strongest possible support to their conclusion. That is, the conclusion of the argument follows inescapably or necessarily from the premises. So obvious is this in each example that anyone accepting (affirming) the premises as true and rejecting (denying) the conclusions as false might be easily suspected of being either mad or else just playful.

Arguments where premises and conclusions are related in this manner are said to be deductively valid, or, more simply, valid. So, to say that an argument is valid is to say that if we affirm its premises we cannot, on pain of absurdity, deny its conclusion. Another way of putting this is to say that, in a valid argument, if the premises are true, then the conclusion must absolutely be true; in no way can it possibly be false.

Our natural reasoning abilities enable us to say that these sample arguments are impeccably valid—that is, that if their premises are true, their conclusions must be true. Saying exactly what makes them so, however, is a very different and far more difficult affair. So, let us go on a bit longer and see where further reflection takes us on this question.

We start by asking, Just why is the validity that we sense, or as we might say, "intuit," in any of these arguments so compelling? What makes it utterly impossible for the conclusions in these arguments to be false if the premises are true? What sense of "impossible" do we have here?

A daring explanation suggests itself. Can it be that the conclusion of a deductively valid argument essentially does nothing more than repeat a claim that is already hidden, i.e., implicitly contained, in the premises? This, if true, would certainly take the mystery out of deductive necessity, i.e., out of the necessary connection between premises and conclusion. For in such a case, it would be patently inconsistent to affirm the premises and at the same time deny them by denying the conclusion.

Okay, let's examine our first example to see if the premises of the argument do in fact implicitly "contain" the conclusion.

> If Bob is wise, he will be cautious.
> But, Bob is wise.
> *Therefore*
> He will be cautious

This argument has two premises:

> If Bob is wise, he will be cautious.
> and
> Bob is wise.

The conclusion of the argument is

> Bob will be cautious.

Now let's do a bit of logical analysis of the premises, that is, take a real close-up look at what they say:

The first premise essentially denies that Bob is both wise and incautious. According to the second premise, Bob *is* wise. Now, all this means that Bob cannot be incautious, simply because that would make him both wise and incautious, in violation of the first premise, which forecloses this possibility. Taken together, therefore, our premises deny that Bob will be incautious which, of course, is precisely equivalent to affirming that he will be cautious. And this is exactly what the conclusion tells us.

Note that in analyzing the premises, we did not simply "pluck out" the conclusion as an explicit component which could be seen to be there by direct inspection. Instead, we paraphrased the premises on the basis of how we understood them. By so doing, we showed indirectly that at least a part of what the premises said was exactly what the conclusion said. And as we have already noted, it is for this reason that the conclusion follows necessarily (i.e., on pain of contradiction) from the premises.

A similar analysis can be made of our second example:

> Either Socrates wanted fame or he wanted justice.
> Fame he did not want.
> *Therefore*
> He wanted justice.

The first premise essentially denies the possibility that he wanted neither fame nor justice. The second premise denies that he wanted fame, which then rules out that he did not want justice. For this would violate the first premise which forbids his wanting neither fame nor justice. Denying that he did not want justice is a double negative and therefore equivalent to affirming that he wanted justice—which is exactly what the conclusion of the argument says.

For conciseness, we analyzed only the two very simplest of our examples and will refrain from going into a similar analysis of the others. Indeed, the last four of our examples would require a much more involved and tedious discussion.

THE DEDUCTIVE CIRCLE

Now, does the fact that a deductively derived conclusion is already contained in the premises make deduction circular and trivial? Circular, yes, but trivial, no!

There are, true enough, perfectly valid deductive arguments which from most practical viewpoints anyone would judge not only circular but quite trivial and even silly, as, for example, the following two:

> Among the citizens of Athens, Socrates was one of the
>   shortest.
> *Therefore*
> Among the citizens of Athens, Socrates was one of the
>   shortest.

Impeccably valid but utterly trivial.

Among his fellows Socrates was the shortest. But with his
   intellect he towered above most men.
Therefore
With his intellect Socrates towered above most men.

Again, absolutely valid and almost as trivial.

LESS OBVIOUS DEDUCTIONS

Our examples of deductive reasoning, so far, while not all quite
trivial, are so simple as to be obviously valid, but some of the
deductive arguments we occasionally give or encounter in pur-
suing our affairs are neither obvious nor trivial. Their conclusions,
like all deductive conclusions, are "contained" in their premises.
But this is far from evident on direct inspection.

There are exactly seven homes on our block. At least one
person lives in each of them, but no more than three persons
live in any one of them. Therefore, there are at least three
homes with the same number of persons living in them.

In a pulp fiction spoof of murder mysteries, one can imagine
an argument like the following:

If the butler was an accomplice then the chauffeur was also
one. And if the chauffeur was, then the wine steward would
have confessed. Now, either the butler was an accomplice or
the gardener was lying. And if the butler was an accomplice
then he would have quit his job. Also, if the butler had quit and
the gardener was lying, then if the fire chief had asked questions, the wine steward would have confessed. But the wine
steward did not confess and the fire chief did ask questions.
Therefore, the chauffeur was an accomplice.

This complex deductive argument is so convoluted as to be
amusing. It is, however, impeccably valid, though not obviously

so. Demonstrating its validity by informal paraphrasing and content analysis could be a rather messy affair. Such an analysis calls for the techniques of modern deductive logic, which it would not be profitable for us to go into here.

DEDUCTIVE CONCLUSIONS AS DISCOVERIES

We see then, that though complex deductive arguments are "circular" (in the sense that their premises implicitly contain their conclusions), they are not viciously circular. That is, they are not "short circuits." In a profound and very important sense, their conclusions are discoveries: something "new" we might not have "seen" without the help of detailed analysis. How trivial or obvious is this familiar argument?

> Your bank certificate of deposit is rated at 6.40 percent, compounded daily. Therefore, the effective annual yield will be 6.60 percent.

Deductive conclusions, therefore, constitute "new" knowledge in two important senses: As a result of the deduction (1) we know something about what the premises imply, and (2) just in case we happen to know that the premises are true, our deduced conclusion constitutes a truth that we were not aware of before the deduction and that we can now believe.

The conclusions of very complex deductive arguments can be very surprising, even astounding, to all concerned, even though they are already implicit in the premises. In such cases, the conclusions are so "deeply hidden" as to be inaccessible by direct inspection, that is, without the help of deductive methods such as we find in formal logic and mathematics. The history of these subjects is largely a history of the development of methods of validly deriving conclusions from premises, or, as some might prefer to say, "proving" conclusions on the basis of premises and valid deductive steps.

Even with such methods in place, showing the deductive validity of some arguments can take a very long time to work out—it has taken years to complete some proofs. For example, though the argument which follows has only one premise, and a simple one at that, no one has yet been able to figure out whether it is deductively valid. (In reading this argument, bear in mind that it does not matter how many humans there are at the moment living on our planet, and that a prime number is a number with no integral factors other than itself and one—as, for example, the numbers, 2, 3, 5, 7, 11, 13, 17, 19, and 23.)

> Twice the number of humans presently living on our planet is an even number greater than 2. Therefore, this number must be the sum of two prime numbers.

This is a special case of a famous conjecture by the mathematician Christian Goldbach (1742), which says that every even integer greater than 2 is the sum of two prime numbers. No one has yet been able to prove this mathematically, which is the same as saying that no one has yet been able to show the following argument to be deductively valid:

> X is any even number greater than 2. *Therefore,* X is the sum of two primes.

The validity of this argument would have to be shown on the basis of the properties of even numbers. It makes no difference how many humans there are. Twice that number (or, for that matter, twice any other natural number) is an even number and that's what matters. If we knew the number of humans then we could no doubt find two primes whose sum equals twice that number. This, however, would only establish the truth of the conclusion. It would not prove the validity of our argument. Putting it differently, it would not show how the conclusion follows logically (deductively) from the premise.

So far, Goldbach's conjecture has held up for all even numbers that have been examined. But until somebody proves it as a theorem, an even number may turn up for which it will fail.

LITTLE STEPS TO FAR OFF PLACES

It is not our purpose here to get into the deductive methods of formal logic and I will absolutely resist the temptation to do so. For those who are more curious about the subject, however, it is important to highlight the following basic fact: *The techniques of formal logic enable us to construct complex deductive arguments or "proofs" as long strings of little steps, each of which is easily shown to be a valid mini-argument.* The validity of the entire complex argument then rests on the validity of each of the component steps.

The usefulness and beauty of formal logic rests largely on the remarkable fact that to construct such proofs of validity, we need a surprisingly small number of standardized mini-arguments whose forms are very much like the ones we've used as examples. With such simple and seemingly trivial elemental arguments, we can, step by step, demonstrate the validity of even the most incredibly complex deductive arguments. The trick is all in discovering the proper sequence of steps. In the hands of skilled reasoners, therefore, the standard forms (basic mini-arguments) of deductive logic, though childishly simple, are stupendously powerful tools of reasoning.

DEDUCTION AND TRUTH

We have already seen that if the premises of a deductively valid argument are all true, then the conclusion must also be true. Another way of putting this is to say that deduction is truth-preservative.

Let's stay with this most remarkable property of deduction a moment longer. It absolutely guarantees the truth of any conclusion that has been deduced from true premises. This means that, starting with true premises, we can set up a deductive argument of whatever length and complexity we please. And, provided we proceed cautiously by small, valid steps so that the entire argument is valid, we need never worry about the truth of the conclusion. It will necessarily be true. Remarkable indeed!

DEDUCTIVE ARGUMENTS WITH FALSE PREMISES

A rather natural question bubbles up here, one that may have occurred to you already: Does deduction also preserve falsity? Or, putting it a little differently, if we deduce any conclusion from false premises must that conclusion also be false? I have asked many students who have never studied logic this question, and the answer has almost always been yes. The correct answer, no, therefore, seems to be counter-intuitive.

Before going further, let us agree that when we say the premises of an argument are true, we mean that they are all true. If this is not the case—if there is even one false premise—then the premises considered as a whole will be said to be false.

Consider the following examples:

> All Frenchmen are great scientists.   (false)
> Lavoisier was French.   (true)
> *Therefore*
> Lavoisier was a great scientist.   (true)

In this example, the falsity of the premises (the first premise is false) is not preserved; that is, it is not transmitted to the conclusion despite the fact that the deduction is impeccably valid.

Another example:

> All Frenchmen are great scientists.   (false)
> Newton was French.   (false)
> *Therefore*
> Newton was a great scientist.   (true)

In this impeccably valid argument, though both premises are false, the conclusion is true.

These last two examples show that a valid argument can have false premises (i.e., premises at least one of which is false) and yet have a true conclusion. Clearly, then, *deduction does not preserve falsity.*

Still, as we might well imagine, deduction from false premises does sometimes lead to a false conclusion. A simple example easily establishes this possibility:

All Frenchmen are great scientists.	(false)
Washington was French.	(false)
Therefore	
Washington was a great scientist.	(false)

Well, what, in final analysis, can we say about valid deductive arguments with false premises? Simply this: When an argument is deductively valid but has false premises, i.e., has at least one false premise, we cannot count on the conclusion one way or the other. It can be either true or false. Or, putting it a little differently and a bit more generally: Deductive arguments tell us nothing about the truth (or falsity) of their conclusions until we know the truth-status of their premises.

This is the most important of our results about deduction so far. It is the starting point of our claim, developed in the next chapter, that for the growth of human knowledge we need something more than deduction.

THE OLDEST OF ALL "LOGICAL" MYTHS

Traditionally, deduction has been closely associated with certainty and truth because deductively valid arguments "certainly" guarantee truth, *provided we start with truth.* It is but a short step from this to a widely held misconception: that the deductive process, in and by itself, and unlike all other kinds of thinking, can, when perfectly valid, somehow bestow certainty and therefore truth on any of its conclusions. Deduction has been seen as the genuine kind of reasoning, the privileged pathway of all analytical thinking, the ultimate logical process for arriving at true conclusions. This idea has no doubt been bolstered by the spectacular success of deduction in mathematics and the other formal sciences.

This time-honored view, however, is little more than a myth. It is, in a profound sense, misguided. As we have already seen, the deductive correctness (validity) of any argument cannot by itself guarantee that the conclusion of that argument will be true—except in one sense only.

Obviously, to any valid deductive argument whose premises are P and whose conclusion is C, we can always attach an additional conclusion. We can always tack on the purely logical truth that C follows necessarily from P. That is, we can "validly" say that the conclusion of our argument follows deductively from its premises. Every valid deductive argument—by itself—entitles us to this much truth, but certainly to no more. In our logical toolbox, therefore, we must have some means of surmounting this deficit; we sorely need a nondeductive manner of reasoning.

Aristotle did write about another kind of thinking for generating truth. He called it *epagoge,* later translated into the Latin as "induction." Very much later, a few Renaissance scholars also protested against the exclusive fixation on deduction. The grip of the deductive myth, however, was not broken until sixteenth-century philosopher Francis Bacon blew the first loud whistle on it, and it was not until John Stuart Mill (1806–1873) and Charles Sanders Peirce (1839–1914) that logic textbooks began to give a significant amount of space to nondeductive modes of reasoning.

SOUNDNESS: Validity with True Premises

We have seen that although a deductive argument is impeccably valid, it can be defective in a very important sense. Its premises may not all be true, in which case they cannot guarantee the truth of the conclusion. And so we call the argument *unsound* despite its deductive validity.

Recall the times when you brusquely interrupted the author of such an argument because "he was off to a false start"? You interrupted in an attempt to save time and effort. And very often, interrupting such an argument can do just that.

A HUGELY POWERFUL, KNOCKDOWN ARGUMENT

By this time, an important and interesting possibility may have come up in your mind, namely, a strategy for establishing or "proving" the possible *falsity* of a claim. The strategy consists of starting with that claim as a premise and then validly deducing a conclusion from it. You then test this conclusion, rather than the original claim, for truth or falsity. If it turns out to be in fact false, then the original claim must also be false; if it were true, our conclusion would also have to be true.

Another, perhaps more useful, way of putting this is to say, as we have already done in our discussion of validity, that *if a deductively valid argument has a false conclusion then it must have at least one false premise.* The premises must contain at least one falsehood, which is equivalent to saying that the premises—considered as one composite claim—must be false.

The method we have just outlined is a powerful strategy for testing any claim whatever, regardless of whether it is a scientific or day-to-day one. Let me illustrate with a simple example: Imagine for a moment that you are vaguely recalling how tall, relative to each other, your three friends are. Your impression is that Barbara is taller than Celarent and Celarent is taller than Darie, but this is at best only a likely supposition. You would like to be sure. Celarent, however, is away. Barbara and Darie, on the other hand, are nearby and can easily be reached. Now, from your supposition that Barbara is taller than Celarent and Celarent is taller than Darie, it follows deductively that Barbara is taller than Darie. But this conclusion can be easily checked directly with the cooperation of both Barbara and Darie, both of whom are available. If it turns out that, in fact, Barbara is not taller than Darie, then your supposition must also be false. For if that supposition were true, any consequence or conclusion deductively drawn from it would also have to be true. Deduction, we recall, is truth-preservative.

As another example, imagine having some reason to believe that an acquaintance of yours, Ferio, was somehow mentally disadvantaged. From this conjecture about Ferio's mental powers, together with a second premise, namely, the fact that no one so disadvantaged is ever admitted to officers' training school (OTS), it follows deductively that Ferio could not have been admitted to OTS. To your surprise, it turns out, however, that he was in fact admitted. The premises of your argument, therefore, must contain a falsehood. This means either that Ferio is not handicapped or else that it is false that those so handicapped are never admitted to OTS. If you could know that your assumption about the admissions policies of OTS was unexceptionably true, thus ruling out corruption or an admissions error, you would have to conclude that your conjecture about Ferio's mental powers was false.

By this time you may be wondering what the point of all this is. Why not test the original claim in the first place? Why bother with a deduced consequence of it—which eventually you must test anyway? One answer is that, as in our Barbara example, it may not be possible, at the moment, to test the original claim. More importantly, the deduced consequence is often a lot simpler than the original claim (premise), which may be quite complex. (Recall that a deduced conclusion is, in general, only a part of the premises.) In our second example, finding out whether or not Ferio was admitted to OTS is probably a lot simpler than our testing his mental capacity.

This is why testing by falsifying a deductive conclusion is so enormously important in the theoretical sciences, where theories and other hypotheses can be very general and very abstract—and therefore highly compressed. When used in science, the knock-down method we have been talking about is known as the hypo-thetico-deductive method. The investigator validly deduces from her theory some simple consequence which can then be easily tested experimentally. If experiment shows this consequence to be false, then the hypothesis, no matter how complex or profound, contains some falsehood. It must therefore be considered false as a whole (assuming, of course, that any hidden assumption she is making in her deduction is not the problem by being itself false).

For example, until the nineteenth century many physicists favored the idea that light travels through empty space in absolutely straight lines. A simple consequence of this hypothesis is that light will cast sharp shadows. Therefore, if we allow light of one color to fall on an opaque screen that has a narrow slit cut into it and we place a second screen behind the first one, we should get a nice, clearly defined sharp image of the slit on the second screen.

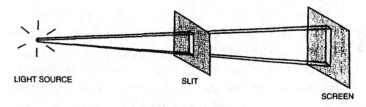

LIGHT SOURCE   SLIT

SCREEN

What we would see on the second screen would look like this:

But this consequence of our straight-line-motion hypothesis turns out to be quite false, as was shown in several famous optical experiments by some early nineteenth-century physicists like Thomas Young and A. G. Fresnel. What they saw instead

was a somewhat fuzzy-edged pattern of bright and dark bands
looking something like this:

The claim or hypothesis that light travels in absolutely straight
lines must therefore be false. This is so, of course, provided we
grant a few (collateral) assumptions about the experimental set-
ups used and some well-established beliefs about things in general.

Incidentally, this falsification happens to have been enormously important in the history of science. It helped settle a long
dispute—for a while, at least—about whether light was a stream
of particles or a train of waves. Particles would cast sharp shadows; waves would not.

Our knockdown method of falsification is invaluable not
only in the sciences but also in other areas of more or less complex investigation such as "sleuthing" and accident analysis.

In a famous rape case of a few years ago, the prosecutor's
claim was that the alleged victim gave no consent. This claim,
together with several general assumptions about how individuals
conduct themselves in such situations, led the jury to the conclusion that there should have been traces of violence—torn clothing
or other such evidence—at the locus of the crime. In fact, such a
conclusion turned out to be largely false; the alleged victim's
clothing showed no such traces. Assuming the truth of all other
(collateral) assumptions that might have been made in this inference, the no-consent hypothesis would have to be judged false and
the rape suspect acquitted. The jury therefore had to decide
whether to reject the no-consent claim of the prosecution or else
brand as false some collateral assumption that may have been
made in the reasoning. What is certain as a matter of logical necessity is that one of these had to be false since the deduced conclu-

sion about traces of violence turned out false. The jury rejected the no-consent charge and acquitted the defendant.

Okay, you are convinced that a false deductive conclusion decisively falsifies the premises. You are also prepared to agree, at least formally, that a true deductive conclusion establishes neither the truth nor the falsity of the premises since even false premises can validly yield true conclusions. By now, though, you are no doubt impatient with the following question: When a hypothesis deductively yields a conclusion that turns out to be true, don't we say that it has been "confirmed" and therefore made somewhat probable?

Yes, we do in fact say that a hypothesis becomes more and more probable as more and more of its deductive consequences turn out to be true—with, of course, none turning out false. But this is not to say that our hypothesis is therefore true. It remains entirely possible that any hypothesis "confirmed" and therefore made "probable" in this way will, after all, still turn out to be false.

*   *   *

Our discussion of deduction has been quite brief, focusing mainly on the essential nature of deductive validity and its relationship to truth. We go now to our next chapter for the kind of reasoning which gets most of our attention in this book because it plays the major role in everyday thinking. This is reasoning of the nondeductive sort. Most logicians call it *inductive* reasoning, and we might as well follow in this tradition.

14

BEYOND DEDUCTION:
The Inductive Leap

THE GROWTH OF KNOWLEDGE:
Deduction Is Not Enough

In everyday living, reasoning is, for the most part, something different from the tidy deductive forms we encountered in the last chapter. It is investigative and creative; its conclusions practical, but more or less uncertain. Sometimes simple, sometimes utterly complex, it indulges in what we might call "intelligent guessing" in order to make some sense of things, discover the causes of what has already happened, and predict what has not yet happened.

> How is it that Howie is spending so much time in his room these days? Is he going to pass math this term?
>
> What could have caused that tragic plane crash?
>
> Will my husband be at the station when I arrive?

The reasoning needed to answer questions like these must at some point be inductive in form. Or, putting it more generally: Deduction alone is not enough to yield the knowledge we need in order to live well and to understand our surroundings.

Let's see why.

REGRESSING FOREVER

In the last chapter we saw that any conclusion obtained by deduction is guaranteed to be true provided we start with premises that are themselves true. Ah, if only we could establish our beliefs by deducing them from true premises, they would then have to be true. This has been the pipe dream of countless thinkers of the past. The dream, however, always runs aground on one hard shoal. Where do we get the true premises? Putting it a little differently, how do we ever get to know that any premise we start with is true?

We could try to deduce our premise from other premises which we already know to be true. But then the question repeats itself: How did we establish the truth of these other premises? Here we're caught in an unending backward chain that philosophers refer to as an infinite regress. There is only limited consolation, therefore, in knowing that starting with true premises, we can, by valid deduction, always arrive at true conclusions.

Worse still, we also recall from the last chapter that a deductive argument starting with true premises guarantees the truth of its conclusion only because that conclusion is already an implicit part of the premises—a part which we extract from the whole, by deductive analysis, and finally exhibit as an explicit conclusion.

Deduction, therefore, gives us no fundamentally new conclusions. It elaborates and calls our attention to content we already implicitly have in our premises, surprising though this content may be once we uncover it as some deductive conclusion. If we are to cope, therefore, with our ever-changing surroundings, understand more about them, and anticipate further change, we need more. Our conclusions must take us beyond our premises, and this means we must go beyond deduction. We must, as it were, break out of the "deductive trap." We need fresh discovery.

THE INDUCTIVE BREAKOUT
AND THE GROWTH OF KNOWLEDGE

Philosophers have never been entirely agreed on exactly what this "breakout" might be. Some have claimed that we naturally have a special, "intuitive" ability to peer into the blizzard of events that engulfs us and come up with some final, rock-bottom truths that need no further validation and that can be the starting points of more reasoning. The trouble with this is that some truths in various areas of knowledge (mathematics included), once thought to be intuitively obvious and therefore final later turned out to be embarrassingly false.

One thing, however, is for sure: As we course through life, we establish a vast portion of our countless beliefs by appealing to what we experience with our senses. And whatever the act is that fixes our beliefs, it can at least be represented as an argument-type move—a nondeductive or, as we shall call it, inductive kind of reasoning. This move takes us from experiential evidence to a conclusion which may be a prediction or an educated guess (explanation) about what is going on behind the appearances.

Asked why I believe that flames are hot or that the sky in fair weather is blue or that Leningrad is now called St. Petersburg, I would reply: I believe it because I have touched some flames or because I have seen the sky countless times or because I have read in many places of the renaming of Leningrad. Even if asked why it is faster, all other things being equal, to get to some destination by traveling in a straight line rather than in a zig-zag, I would say that I have seen this to be so in all my attempts to move toward any destination whatsoever.

That we can be said to reason in this fashion in order to justify beliefs is nowadays hardly a matter of contention. Our language certainly reflects this. For, in reporting what we learn from experience we connect with that experience by using terms such as "because," "since," "given that," and "therefore" just as we do in the case of any other kind of reasoning.

There is, however, one proviso: No conclusion based on experience can ever be final. It always remains possible, in principle, that the very next experience will be surprisingly different and require us to doubt that conclusion.

THE STRENGTH OF INDUCTIVE ARGUMENTS

In the course of living, we secure a vast store of beliefs. About some of these we feel very certain, as, for example, that each of us will die sooner or later, or that the earth is round. About others we may have considerable doubt, as, for example, that human history is shaped mostly by economics, or that drinking hot tea and whisky is a good remedy for a cold. If we are reasonable persons, the confidence we have in these beliefs depends upon how compelling the evidence for them is, which is the same as saying that confidence depends on how strong our inductive arguments for them are. The strengths of inductive arguments can vary over a wide range, and judging these strengths is the major task in all inductive reasoning.

Fortunately, we are rather good at this sort of thing and can often estimate the strength of an argument without much thought. The amount of evidence reported in the premises is a major consideration. For example, we easily judge the following argument to have little if any strength at all:

> I have met a total of four North Dakotans and they have all
> been good-natured.
> *Therefore (Probably)*
> The very next one I meet will be good-natured.

If we consider for a moment the negation of the conclusion of this argument, namely, "The next North Dakotan I meet will not be good-natured," we can judge this negation to be a close rival of the positive conclusion in the sense that it is only slightly less plausible. Given the scanty evidence, the chance that the positive conclusion is true is not much greater than that of its negative rival.

Here is one that is so weak as to be silly and hardly to be taken seriously:

> My cab-driver, this first morning in Paris, was brusque.
> *Therefore (Probably)*
> The very next one will (also) be brusque.

By contrast consider the following example:

> Every one of the hundreds of lemons I have ever tasted has
> been sour.
> *Therefore (Probably)*
> The very next one will be sour.

In this argument the premise gives very strong support to the conclusion, making it very probable, though never absolutely certain. For, though the premise may be true, the conclusion may still be false. I don't need a logician's skill to see this. It is entirely possible for me to have tasted hundreds of lemons, all of them sour, and eventually to come upon one that is not. It so happens, by the way, that there in fact are such lemons, not usually grown commercially. They are lemons which are sweet, though externally indistinguishable from sour ones.

We can put all this another way: Any expectation that the next lemon will not be sour would certainly be unreasonable or, as we might say, implausible. But such an expectation does not flatly contradict the fact (premise) that all my past lemons have been sour. My premise and my bizarre expectation could both turn out to be true no matter how surprising this combination of outcomes might be.

BACKGROUND KNOWLEDGE AND RELEVANCE

In judging the strength of an inductive argument, we take into account not only the amount of evidence reported in the premises but also "how tightly" it connects with the conclusion. To judge this "tightness" or *relevance,* as it is also called, we need to know something about the subject matter of our reasoning. That is, we need to draw on our background knowledge of how the things we're reasoning about relate to each other.

Here is an example in which the mere "quantity" of evidence appears to be, in some sense, small, but the bearing it has on the conclusion is considerable:

> All of Susan's relatives have myopia.
> *Therefore (Probably)*
> Susan has myopia.

In this argument the premises have rather limited content. Yet the argument is strong by virtue of the background knowledge we can bring to it. We know that myopia is to some extent congenital, that is, those who have myopia in their families are rather likely to have the condition themselves.

Another example:

> Senator Strom Thurmond has survived his ninety-fifth birthday.
> *Therefore (Probably)*
> He will survive his next one.

This argument has essentially the very same form as the sour lemon one with about the same sort and range of supporting evidence in the premise, but the argument is weaker because we know that only a modest fraction of even healthy ninety-five-year-olds make it to their next birthday. This sets the likelihood that Thurmond will celebrate his next birthday at something less than the likelihood that my next lemon will be sour.

The strength of our birthday argument is greatly reduced by another, one might say "higher" or more sweeping, induction. We are reminded here of the fabled chicken who, having no background knowledge about what chicken farmers do, went confidently to the hand that had fed it every day for the past six months and did itself in.

Some more examples:

> Some investment managers attempting to attract investors never tire of proclaiming that their stock funds have yielded spectacular returns (as much as 25 percent) for the past year. The implied inference is that a similar return should be expected for next year. What they never tell us is that all bull markets in the past have eventually turned bearish and that the present stock market could be a very mature bull.

> On a backpacking trip last year, I brushed against an unfamiliar vine and soon got a nasty rash where it touched me. Hiking somewhere else, I now see a vine which looks a lot like the one I touched last year. Its leaves are also deeply scored, shiny, and bright green.
> *Therefore (Probably)*
> If I touch it I will again get a rash.

This is a fairly strong argument. Still, despite my experience with last year's vine, it remains entirely possible that if I touch this one I will not get a rash. It would no doubt be reckless for me to accept the premise of this argument and yet reject its conclusion. Doing so would most certainly not land me in a contradiction (as would be the case if my argument were deductive). It would be surprising but not absurd to find that after touching the second vine I got no rash.

> My sister-in-law in recent months has not reciprocated our invitations. She has never come to our home except at our invitation and, on such occasions, has been generally disagreeable, seeming to take every opportunity to be critical and disapproving of everything we do or own. She never

smiles good naturedly, and she responds negatively to
every attempt on our part to reach out to her.
Therefore (probably)
She does not value our friendship and wishes to keep as much
distance as possible between our two households.

This time, the conclusion is a little more uncertain. Another
plausible account of my sister-in-law's behavior might be that
she is having emotional problems (perhaps bordering on serious
depression) which make her indifferent to much of what is going
on around her. Or she may be beset by other stressful factors in
her own immediate circumstances.

*   *   *

We have just introduced inductive reasoning with a few scattered
examples. Let us now consider three basic forms of this kind of
thinking. We'll start with the two simplest and most natural
forms of it in our next chapter.

15

ANALOGY AND FORECAST:
Early Moves

THE ART OF ANALOGY

Two friends are at a wedding feast and looking at an assortment of tempting preprandial snacks that an engaging waitress is serving on a small tray. One of them asks her: "What are these ring-shaped things?" He is looking at irregularly shaped ringlets that seemed deep-fried. The waitress answers, "Squid." As the wedding guest clears his throat, the other cuts in, "Try them! I was here last month for Meg's wedding, and had some things that looked very much like these. If I remember correctly, it was this very same woman that served them, possibly in the very same carved wood tray. Yes, she called them 'squid.' They were absolutely delicious!"

The guest is reasoning by analogy. That is, he compares the exotic appetizers before him with some others which he tasted recently, which looked very much like these, and which he found to be very pleasing. On the basis of visible similarities he then concludes that they are also similarly pleasing.

I remember vividly how, as a child, I felt the unsettling pinch of a sand crab as it started up my leg one day at the beach and how a day later in the park I recoiled in dread of a large spider. This, again was an analogy, but this time not quite as structured. The inference, if there was one, was undeliberate, almost knee-jerk, but we can reasonably reconstruct it as not very different from the one in the fried squid example, except for the immediacy with which it occurred. On the basis of the strong resemblances between the two multilegged creatures, I felt (concluded) that the spider would be as "pinchy" and unsettling as the crab.

Our backpacking story about two roadside vines is still another example. This time the reasoning is a lot more deliberate. The two plants were alike in a number of obvious respects. Both were vinelike, with green shiny leaves of similar shape. The first plant caused a rash on contact with my arm. Given the obvious similarities between the two plants, I then concluded that the second would also cause a rash if I touched it.

And now for a more carefully structured analogy drawn by scientific researchers: Laboratory mice eat just about the same food as humans do, and they metabolize their nutrients in comparably similar fashion. When aniline dyes are put in their food, a lot more of them get bladder cancer than otherwise. On the basis of these physiological resemblances investigators believe that aniline dyes can also be carcinogenic for humans.

As is clear from our examples, in reasoning by analogy, we conclude that something has a certain property on the grounds that something else which is similar also has that property. The two entities involved are called analogs.

Although analogs must be similar in some respects, they will also differ in others. Mice are very much smaller than humans: They mature and reproduce far faster than humans; they have different body temperatures and shapes from humans; and so on. The two vines in my backpacking story were very similar in virtually all visible respects, but they weren't quite the same size. And, of course, they grew in different locations. I might add, one grew on low, moist ground, the other on a high, generally drier spot.

The more similar two analogs are the more stock we tend to place in the analogy we draw between them. This seems to be a reasonable thing to do. When the analogs have many properties in common, they are likely to have the same kind of underlying structures producing the similarities we observe. Differences between analogs, of course, tend to undermine our confidence in the analogy, and the more the differences, the weaker we judge the analogy.

There is, however, an important qualification in all this: The similarities and differences we take into consideration must be relevant ones. Deciding on this relevance can be a tricky matter.

Two things which seem very different may, in certain relevant respects, in fact be very similar. Recall the obvious differences between mice and men in FDA studies or between dummies and humans in car crash experiments. Mechanical and electrical set-ups can look very different, yet engineers use electrical analogs to analyze mechanical systems. And just how important is the much shorter lifespan of the mouse in drawing analogies to humans? And what about its metabolic rate and body temperature? Does the fact that the deadly poisonous mushroom which our hiking guide pointed to had flaky scales on its cap justify our abjuring the next mushroom with flaky scales on its cap?

To make these judgments of relevance we fall back, once again, on our background knowledge which, in day-to-day situations, is the best guide we have.

As most of us know, The fact that both plants were vines surely seems relevant. It could put us on the track to deciding that both plants were of the same species. We would likewise judge other structural and color similarities relevant on the basis of knowing that the visible characteristics of a plant are generally good clues to the sort of plant it is. We also know, however, that a number of other similarities, such as the fact that both plants were growing by the side of the road or that both were growing under a Norwegian maple, have no bearing on the analogy.

The same sort of considerations apply on more technical levels to FDA testing with mice. Once we learn of the physiological similarities of the mouse to the human, we see that they are strongly relevant. But the facts that, like humans, mice are very competitive, learn the maze rather quickly, and are mortal we easily discount as having little bearing on the analogy.

Differences must also be ruled out or counted in as relevant. That the stems of one plant might have been red and those of the other were not would have been relevant. But that one plant was somewhat larger than the other, or that one was growing on high ground and the other on low ground, most likely would not.

And, as the experts tell us about the mice-humans analogy, differences like the fact that mice are not primates, or that their metabolic rates are considerably higher, or that their lifespans are very much shorter do tend to weaken the analogy, while their being much smaller, their having tails, and their having much harder front teeth have little bearing on it.

THE EASE OF DRAWING ANALOGIES:
Jump-Start Reasoning

For the most part, reasoning by analogy comes to us with great facility. We tend to draw analogies on the slightest similarity. Typically, this mode of reasoning does not embroil us in more or less complex scenarios, as diagnostic reasoning often does. Nor does it call for a large number of cases, as does *simple prediction,* which we will discuss next. Instead, analogies rest on rather scanty premises, namely, what we know about the two analogs. The rest is a matter of gauging the relevance of similarities and differences.

Analogies, therefore, are a ready and frequently used form of argument and can serve superbly as jump-starters or as auxiliary devices in wider contexts of reasoning. We draw analogies in this way—often successfully—on all levels of reasoning, from the simplest playtime contexts to the most arcane scientific and philosophical ones. Indeed, we do some of our most productive analogical thinking without much deliberation and often without being aware that we're doing it.

We need hardly say by now that analogies are inductive arguments. No matter how similar two analogs may appear to be, the unlikely can still happen. They can still turn out to be different with respect to some property of interest to us.

AVOIDING FLABBY THINKING

Unfortunately, the ease with which we draw analogies is the very reason our analogies are often too weak to give much support to our conclusions. This happens when the similarity is too little or else irrelevant. To the untrained eye, two mushrooms may look entirely alike, yet one will be harmless and the other deadly. Two gases may each be colorless, odorless, and tasteless, yet one will sustain you and the other will kill you. Our science fiction stories are replete with electronically wired robots that reason, react, and look like humans but, unlike humans, feel no pain, joy, desire, or anything else.

The facility with which we can draw analogies, together with their risky nature, make it advisable to use this kind of reasoning only with the utmost caution and preferably at only the early stages of conjecture. In this way, they remain subject to further investigation and hopeful confirmation. The crucial step in the reasoning is the judgment of relevance. Critical alertness and familiarity with the subject matter are crucial in drawing plausible analogies, but the fact that the judgments of relevance can be so tricky often makes it advisable to bring in the knowledge of experts in order to safeguard a dubious analogy.

> Oh yes, a friend of mind recently had the very same kind of large lump on her neck. She recovered by wearing a kerchief for several weeks to keep her neck warm during sleep. So for now, don't bother with doctors, and don't worry. Just do what my friend did, and you'll come through it fine the way she did.

One needs little common sense to know that in this case a doctor, the expert, most certainly should be consulted. Still, the great facility with which we draw analogies has made them enormously productive in triggering thought even at the most general and abstract levels of human inquiry. Indeed, they have helped create some of the greatest theories in the history of science from antiquity to the very present. In our next chapter, we will see how drawing an analogy could have triggered the chain of reasoning that led the ancient Greeks to the first great theory of matter, the atomic theory. In chapter 20 and elsewhere we will mention the role of analogy in scientific thinking, to describe, for example, how Einstein may have arrived at the special theory of relativity.

We all owe at least *one* great belief to analogy: How would you know that your companion is in pain except by analogy with the things you say, the sounds you make, and all the other things you do when you, yourself, are in pain? Indeed, would you know that she has any feelings or thoughts or any mental life whatever if not for similar analogies?

Analogy has no doubt played a key role in the growth of human knowledge from its most primitive beginnings to its most advanced stages. When we consider that there is an element of analogy in every metaphor we utter and in every positive comparison we make, it would hardly be preposterous to suggest that drawing analogies is the most facile and pervasive form of reasoning—possibly, the first and most open gateway to human knowledge.

SIMPLE PREDICTION: Primitive Knowledge

Imagine that you are observing the effects of a certain Chinese herb that a friend has recommended for your after-breakfast heartburn. You know virtually nothing about the therapeutic value of herbs, much less, Chinese herbs. Also, you have little or no background knowledge about how any substance could possibly work to neutralize stomach acids or to inhibit their production. In fact, you know nothing worth mentioning about the stomach, acids, or, for that matter, the biology of any part of your body whatsoever. You are, as one might say, in the state of primitive knowledge with respect to the stomach and any disorders it may have.

But you have taken the Chinese herb about a dozen times after breakfast and, in each such case, the usual heartburn has not occurred. You're now willing to predict that the very next time you take the herbal tea after breakfast, the heartburn will not occur. In making this prediction on the basis of the several past instances, you have engaged in another primitive kind of inductive reasoning, the kind we are here calling *simple prediction.* The reasoning is of course inductive, because despite the perfect batting average to date, your prediction can still turn out false.

It is difficult to imagine any reasoning more elemental than simple prediction. We have seen that reasoning by analogy can also operate on very elementary levels, but even the most simple analogies, rough and spontaneous though they may be, require us to decide on relevant similarities and differences, and this can call for considerable background knowledge. Essentially, all we do in simple prediction, however, is observe that two kinds of "things" (events, properties, situations) have occurred together several times and, on this basis, expect them to occur together the very next time around.

In such thinking, we flatly assume that all occurrences observed are of exactly the same two kinds, for example, taking herbal tea and having no heartburn, or looking like a lemon and tasting sour, or being a glowing metal and being hot. This assumption is usually made uncritically, simply on the basis of the first blush appearances by which we recognize what we are observing. True, there is an element of analogy in the simple judgments of similarity being made. But typically, only the grossest comparisons for relevant similarities and differences are involved.

It is generally assumed that the occasions on which all occurrences have taken place are so similar that the equivalence of all occurrences is never in doubt. In fact, we say, colloquially and uncritically, that what has happened over and over again is "the very same thing" rather than a string of very similar events. The strength of a simple prediction therefore does not vary essentially with similarities, differences, and relevancies as does the strength of an analogy. It depends essentially on the number of repeated occurrences of the two kinds of events, properties, situations, etc. involved. The greater the number of such occurrences, the more plausible is the prediction.

Further comparing analogy and simple prediction, we might note that they are alike and different in an interesting way. In both, we want some quantity to be large. In analogy, that quantity is the number of relevant similarities between two events; in simple prediction, it is the number of occurrences of "an event."

CORRECTED SIMPLE PREDICTION

Just as we draw better analogies with the help of background knowledge, we can upgrade our simple predictions (after which they are no longer "simple") by bringing in background knowledge to correct and refine them.

For example, I have driven my E-Class Chrysler for about 100,000 miles without major breakdown, and it has gotten me to work every working day throughout every month of those years. On the basis of a simple prediction, I might, on first consideration, want to conclude that I can put another four hundred miles on it over the next month by taking it to work as I have throughout the past ninety-six months. But I also know that E-Class Chryslers hardly ever last for more than 100,000 miles without major breakdown. My prediction, therefore, that it will get me to work without a problem over the next thousand miles is greatly weakened by this background knowledge. I may, therefore,·decide not to risk it and go for a new car while the old one is still running and I can drive it to the dealer for a trade-in.

A similar modification is reasonably applicable in a situation like the following: An Eskimo's prediction that the next bear he sees will be white is reasonable as a prediction made in the state of primitive knowledge and based on the hundreds of bears which he has seen as far back as he can remember and which have all been white. But if he were to widen his travels to take in more southerly latitudes and learn that the color of fur-bearing animals varies considerably, especially when different climates are involved, he would have to reduce the confidence he had in his prediction or perhaps abandon it altogether.

Let's turn once more to the stock market, which has been an investor's dream for the past several years: a raging bull surging to more and more new highs. I, unfortunately, have been on the sidelines during all this time and have lost out on the action. If I jump in now, I can participate in the market gains, perhaps for a good while. The likelihood that this move will be successful, however, is significantly diminished by the fact that I would be first taking a position in an aging bull market whose stock prices, in relation to company earnings, are historically sky high. Indeed, past market cycles give some reason to believe that a substantial correction or downturn could be close at hand. Any induction I make about what the market will do over the next several months, therefore, will certainly not be a *simple* prediction.

Our past examples about nonagenarian birthdays and guileless chickens illustrate the same sort of correction. Simple inductions based on past event-sequences are always subject to correction on the basis of more advanced knowledge, i.e., relevant background knowledge—when, of course, such knowledge is available.

STATISTICAL PREDICTION

Almost as primitive and very similar to simple prediction is *statistical prediction*. The premises in this kind of reasoning report an event-sequence that is only fractionally rather than entirely positive. That is, the reasoning starts with statistical premises, sometimes in terms of percentages, sometimes only roughly as in the following:

> Of the many, many fish ever observed, nearly all (though not all) have been oviparous.

Therefore (Probably)
The new female angler they've just added to the aquarium will
    eventually produce eggs.

Almost everything we said about simple prediction applies to statistical prediction. Notice, however, that not only does the quantity of cases observed strengthen the argument, but also the percentages reported. Obviously if the premises in the above argument had reported only 75 percent of all fish ever observed (instead of nearly all) as oviparous, the resulting argument would have been much weaker.

Statistical predictions are, of course, genuinely inductive kinds of arguments. As in all inductive arguments, the premises confer only probability on the conclusion. It is always possible that chance will not grace our perfectly sound prediction and that the unexpected will occur instead.

In this regard it is worth mentioning a very common error which you'll hear committed even by the (presumably) most sophisticated discussants. Recall how often we angrily and mercilessly condemn the meteorologists who predict rain on an 80 percent chance, and it later turns out not to rain. In fact, those serious and relentlessly working victims of our wrath were not wrong at all, even though we made no use of the monstrous umbrellas we dragged along. Their prediction was a statistical one, no doubt made perfectly reasonable by the statistical premises available to them.

* * *

Having viewed these simple and very natural forms of inductive reasoning, let's turn now to what is probably the most powerful and far-reaching kind all rational thinking. It has no doubt been the key player in the development not only of our common sense legacy of knowledge, but of our scientific culture as well. What is more, it is that mode of reasoning which operates in much of our inventive and creative thinking. So, on to our next chapter for a first look at what we'll call *diagnostic reasoning*.

16

FROM APPEARANCE TO REALITY:
The Diagnostic Plunge

[The diagnostic plunge] permits our hypotheses to die in our stead.

Sir Karl Popper

DIAGNOSTIC REASONING: In Three Steps

One of the most enduring and vulgar prejudices of the ages is the idea that creative thinking and reasoning are utterly incompatible and diametrically opposed. Thinking that is truly creative, we are told, must be of the "divergent" sort (I guess this means of a non-reasoning kind).

No idea is more misguided, and the most dramatic counter-example is diagnostic reasoning, the most complex, most interesting, and most far-reaching form of inductive reasoning. It is the mode of reasoning that has more to do with the growth and depth of human knowledge than any other. Its intensely creative nature will become apparent as we go on.

Philosophers and logicians of the past who have concerned themselves with diagnostic reasoning have called it by a variety of names such as hypothesizing, theorizing, conjecturing, educated guessing, supposing, and so on. The American pragmatist Charles Sanders Peirce (1839–1914) distinguished it from induction and called it *abduction*. But we are here labeling all nondeductive reasoning as inductive, and disagnostic reasoning is nondeductive. We will therefore stay with classifying it as a kind inductive reasoning.

We've already had several simple examples of diagnostic reasoning: At the start of chapter 3 we had one about a lost wallet. Early in chapter 4 we had one concluding that the milk was spoiled and one concluding that Bert had gained weight. Here is a fresh example, this time about an air disaster. It is based on an actual event, but limitations of space have required us to simplify the account considerably.

Some years ago, a Boeing 737 with many passengers aboard crashed mysteriously in Colorado Springs as it came in for a normal landing. There were no survivors. Our question is, Why did the plane crash? (What happened just before that tragic moment?) Answering this question calls for reasoning of the sort we are calling diagnostic. This is reasoning which we can conveniently divide into three steps, the second and third of which usually require expert knowledge.

STEP ONE

What may surprise you about diagnostic reasoning is that though we are not experts, we can, in many cases, make some starts. We can construct a step-one diagnostic argument on the basis of the scenario that presents itself, our own personal knowledge, and a few other background clues of which we may soon become aware. Altogether these will constitute the premises of our step-one diagnostic inference.

Let's give this a try for the Colorado plane crash. What premises can we put together for a start? Well, first we can create a set of claims or statements which itemize all the available information that we think has a significant bearing on the matter.

1. The plane was seen diving almost vertically into the ground at great speed.

2. Six seconds before landing the pilot reported everything okay as he headed for a normal landing.

3. There are mountains not far in the background of the crash area.

4. No aircraft, birds, or other objects were reported in the area.

5. The pilot was a healthy man, thirty-five years old, with eight years of accident-free experience in commercial flying.

6. The plane was three years old with no history of structural or mechanical problems.

Our aim, now, is to come up with the conclusion we want. For the sake of highlighting the crucial points of logic involved, we must go rather slowly in our discussion. In actual practice, your own thinking is likely to be a lot faster and less methodical, so bear with me as we go from one step to the next.

We begin by dipping into our own background where we usually find a rich store of applicable knowledge. Indeed, the amount of background knowledge any one of us possesses on most topics can be hugely surprising. What is more, we are remarkably good at selecting and bringing that knowledge into our reasoning.

One explanation that will surely occur to you at the very outset is that the pilot suffered a stroke just as he nosed down for a landing. Such an explanation would constitute what we sometimes call a hypothesis or theory (also, conjecture or supposition). Terms like these convey the idea that the explanation is subject to more or less doubt and is at best only an "educated guess" made to some extent plausible by the premises we have just listed. It is important to remember that in our own account of this reasoning process we are calling such hypotheses or suppositions "conclusions." Doing so should not convey the idea that what we're calling "conclusions" are in any sense final or even well established. They are, especially in step one, the very tentative and uncertain conclusions of very weak arguments.

How do we gauge the uncertainty in this early account of the accident? In doing this, we inevitably become aware that the stroke hypothesis is not the only one possible. It has some interesting rivals, any of which easily take shape as we reflect more and more on the matter. Here are some (together with our first conclusion):

1. The pilot had a stroke.

2. Some crucial mechanism locked after nosing down for a landing, thus depriving the pilot of control.

3. There was a sudden and powerful downward shift in wind direction which abruptly nosed the plane into the ground as it descended for a landing.

And with some imagination you might easily invent others—some very unlikely or even bizarre but still possible—in some broad enough sense of "possible." A rather implausible one, for example, might be that a suicidal high-jacker had put a gun to the pilot and ordered him to announce his okay message and then nose the plane down. Still more fancifully, one could imagine a mysterious force from some unseen UFO that drove the plane down. These last two conjectures, especially the last one, do so much violence to what we already know about the way things really happen that, though they are *not* "absolutely" impossible, they are too implausible to be given further consideration. No pilot close to the ground would dive vertically down at full speed even under a threat to his life. Hitting the ground vertically at that speed leaves no one any chance of survival. And as for UFOs . . .

We are left, therefore, with three rival conclusions—hypotheses, if you prefer—and are now ready to rank them in order of plausibility. At first glance, all three can seem about equally plausible. On reflection, however, the plausibility of the stroke conclusion drops a notch or two simply because strokes in healthy thirty-five-year-olds are extremely rare, even under great physical stress. Our top rivals, therefore are two: one about locked controls, the other about a powerful wind effect. Our stroke conclusion stays in the running but is lower in our plausibility ranking.

Let us say that, at this point, we have completed a step-one or, as we might also call it, a preliminary *plausibility ranking* of our diagnostic conclusions based only on our personal background knowledge and on the available information about the scenario which immediately presents itself.

We have essentially completed our preliminary plausibility ranking. But it would be nice if, even this early, we can be a bit more quantitative about it by fitting a couple of numbers to our rankings. Taken together, the plausibilities of our three rival conclusions come to nearly 100 percent. These are the only three realistic possibilities. The plausibility or likelihood that the right conclusion is going to be either one or another of them, therefore, is close to certainty. That is, our three rivals cover (practically) the full range of realistic possibilities. We can now think of this "total plausibility" (100 percent) as being divided among the three conclusions in proportion to how their plausibilities compare to each other.

We might, for example, assign a 20 percent plausibility to our low ranker (stroke) and divide the remaining 80 percent between our two top ones (locked controls and wind shift). At this point, we might even want to rank the locked controls conclusion somewhat below the wind shift one because radar sighted no birds, meteorites, or other objects that could have jammed the steering mechanisms. So, we might settle on assigning 45 percent, 35 percent, and 20 percent to the wind shift, locked controls, and stroke conclusions, respectively.

One very important point in all this is that no matter how we fine tune our plausibility allotment to the two high-ranking conclusions, they are pretty close rivals. Their plausibilities, numerically expressed, are close in magnitude. This means that as long as our two high rankers are close, the likelihood of either one being true is too small to be satisfactory. Remember that the available plausibility—about 80 percent—must be closely divided between them.

Obviously, therefore, even though we rank the wind shift hypothesis first, we would most certainly not want to bet on it. For, at 45 percent plausible, it is hardly a 50–50 deal and, is in fact, more likely to be false than true. Of course, if we were absolutely forced to bet on one of the three rivals, the reasonable move would be to bet on the wind shift one. But if we were free to do so, holding off betting would be the reasonable choice. The diagnostic process, therefore, is not finished. It's time for closer investigation, and we must go to step two.

STEP TWO

Closer investigation entails examining the strewn parts of the aircraft more carefully, recovering voice records, reading what is left of the instrument panel, and so on. This second stage of the investigation will therefore require the help of experts and possibly the use of some sophisticated technology such as X-rays of metallic parts to detect metal fatigue, chemical tests, and medical lab analyses. In the case of this unfortunate accident, closer investigation in fact yielded a few more findings which we must add to our original premises as follows:

7. The instrument panel showed a speed of about 160 knots at the time of impact.

8. All ailerons and other controls were found clear of obstructions and properly set for normal landing, not for diving.

9. Experts testified that in areas like Denver and Colorado Springs, with their mountains, climate, etc., a type of air turbulence called "pin-wheel rotor" or "wind shear" has occasionally occurred during the time of the year of the crash. Such rotors can occur at low altitudes and can instantly alter the attitude (tilt) of an aircraft on landing or taking off. This effect can be strong enough to cause a nose-dive crash. Indeed, as the experts reported, over the past two decades, these powerful, deadly gusts have been associated with at least twenty-six aircraft accidents, killing more than 500 people in the United States!

Our step-two inquiries have yielded these additional premises with a significant bearing on the critical plausibilities. The wind shear conclusion gains decisively over the locked controls one. Its plausibility jumps considerably while that of its competitor plummets. The fact that the controls were found unobstructed and fixed for normal landing raises the puzzling question of how they could have, for only a moment, frozen in a nose-dive setting.

The wind shear hypothesis is now substantially more plausible than its competitors. And the reasonable thing to do, therefore, is to regard it, at this point in our reasoning, as the conclusion of a diagnostic argument, which so far consists of nine premises and one conclusion.

STEP THREE

Though the wind shear conclusion is, by now, the most reasonable, its competitor has not dropped so far below it as to free us of all gnawing doubt. Well then, could more have been done? Yes, more could have been done but wasn't. Imagine for example that a very precise miniature simulation or model of the crash area terrain could have been constructed along with the known local atmospheric conditions. Possibly, a miniature pin-wheel rotor (wind shear) of the required type could in this way have been artificially produced and made to bring about a laboratory nose-dive quite analogous to the one of the crash. Such a test or, better still, experiment, could count as very strong corroboration of the pin-wheel rotor conclusion, possibly freeing it of any practical doubt. Another corroboration would have been secured if the records of some local weather station somehow showed that pin-wheel rotor air currents had occurred in the area that very day.

At any rate, the diagnostic process should, in general, include a third stage of inquiry, one that we might call the confirmation stage. It would consist of procedures such as crucial laboratory tests or experiments designed to yield highly specific data which could very directly and concretely confirm (or contradict) the conclusion in point. The decisiveness of a confirmation procedure derives from the fact that if the results are positive, they are very precisely what we would expect to get if (and, most likely only if) the conclusion being tested were in fact true. Viewed as part of our final diagnostic argument, these results could be viewed as additional premises in support of our diagnostic conclusion.

In this air accident example, step three never took place simply because a simulation model of the sort we have imagined would have been too difficult and costly to construct. Nor were there any weather bureau records available about local air patterns in Colorado Springs for that day. Investigators, however, could have ordered other, more auxiliary, confirmation procedures. They could for example have done an autopsy on the pilot to rule out stroke or heart attack. And they might have done more sensitive tests on the relevant structures to determine whether any objects had struck and disabled them near the moment of crashing. This could have essentially ruled out or further ruled "down" the frozen flap conclusion.

THE REASONABLE ARGUMENT

Because no solid confirmation procedure was, at that time, practically feasible, the pin-wheel rotor conclusion for the Colorado Springs disaster remained a bit shaky. It was a "very best" conclusion, but far from a sure bet. Still, it was the conclusion of what one might call a *reasonable* argument—namely the argument with the most plausible rival (under the available evidence) as its conclusion. It should be entirely clear by now, however, that, like any other inductive conclusion, the conclusion of this argument—plausible though it was—could never have been absolutely final. It must always have remained tentative pending any new evidence. New evidence could have (and still can) always turn up and alter, perhaps even drastically, the entire array of plausibilities among the original hypotheses. Of course, if step three (confirmation) had been done, our conclusion would have been much more "final." But just how final could this ever have been? Certainly, not absolutely final? After all, our conclusion was still only inductively secured.

The term "diagnosis" is prominent in medical practice, and of course refers to diagnostic reasoning. For medical diagnoses, we, of course, are safest with the medical experts, but we all have some reliable background knowledge on which we can and do often make a rough start, even if only to decide whether or not to see a doctor.

Susan has been complaining for the past couple of days of a pain in the upper back a touch below her left shoulder blade. She now has a fairly high temperature and a dry cough. Her mother looked at Susan's back carefully and noted a few other things. Let us list all of this along with some background facts, as the premises for a possible step-one diagnostic inference:

1. Susan has a stabbing pain in the upper back.

2. She has a high temperature and a dry cough.

3. There is no discoloration or tender spot near the surface of her body.

4. Susan is sixteen years old.

5. She smokes a lot and has done so for about a year.

6. There is no flu epidemic; nor is it the season for one.

7. She has no history of serious illness.

STEP ONE

Susan and her mother have spent some time puzzling over what might be causing Susan's symptoms. Several possibilities came up which we can consider as the possible conclusions of a preliminary or step-one diagnostic argument.

Susan has:

1. a very bad chest cold

2. flu

3. pneumonia

Their conjectures are interrupted by a phone call from a friend who, after asking how Susan was doing, said that tuberculosis was on the rise and should be considered. Knowing that Susan was a heavy smoker, he also suggested lung cancer as another possibility. By this time, Susan's younger brother came in from a basketball game and suggested some sort of trauma-caused injury possibly resulting from Susan's first stint at lacrosse the day before yesterday.

Let's add these considerations to our list of possible conclusions:

4. tuberculosis

5. lung cancer

6. trauma-caused injury

Crude as these guesses may be, Susan's family will no doubt attempt to rank them according to their plausibilities. To begin with, they drop the injury conclusion to a very low position in the ranking because it poses too many other puzzles. It leaves unexplained the fact that Susan's pain does not vary when she moves her arms. Torn muscles and fractured ribs are very painful when we try to move nearby tissues. Also, it fails to explain the cough and the fever, as well as the absence of tender spots and discolorations.

Another rival that immediately drops to low rank is the cancer conclusion. They recall that lung cancer does not seem to afflict young people often and having smoked one year does not have much bearing on the matter.

The tuberculosis hypothesis suffers considerably when Susan's mother points out that although nowadays TB is on the rise, it is in fact still very rare among all but the most disadvantaged people. Susan is of at least middle-class status.

Susan's family are therefore left with the first three conjectures to consider, namely, bad chest cold, flu, or pneumonia. The very bad chest cold possibility is certainly strong but does not quite explain the spiking fever. All those present agree that even chest colds with marked bronchitis are not typically accompanied by such high temperature. And the exquisite, stabbing pains that Susan presents doesn't seem to go with flu, which is not in season anyway. So the flu hypothesis drops down a little, though perhaps not quite as much as the chest cold one. At this level of conjecture, the pneumonia hypothesis is certainly to be taken seriously. It seems to outrank both the flu and the chest cold conclusions. But again, as in the case of the Colorado Springs disaster, it is only the best of three conclusions which are all in the running and among which the total plausibility—roughly 100 percent—must be divided. No one of these three alternatives, therefore, is decisively strong, but all of them are "real" possibilities. The reasoning calls for closer investigation, that is, for second stage, i.e., step two, diagnostic inquiry. The time has come to call a doctor.

STEP TWO

The doctor now examines Susan. He mostly checks her respiratory system: taps her chest and back and listens to her breathing. In addition, he gets chest X-rays.

The sounds the physician hears and the shadows in the X-rays are strongly suggestive of inflammation and fluid in the lungs, i.e., pneumonia. And so, at this point the doctor is willing to say that Susan does have pneumonia. The second stage of diagnostic inquiry, then, strongly indicates pneumonia as, by far, the most plausible conclusion of the diagnostic reasoning—up to this point anyway.

STEP THREE

Although on this basis the doctor goes ahead with antibiotics, he would like to strengthen the argument or inference even more with a confirmation or third-stage diagnostic inquiry. This is the stage of diagnostic reasoning that can make the already very plausible pneumonia conclusion a practical certainty.

In this case, a confirmation procedure is fortunately available, although it requires some sophisticated laboratory techniques. The doctor orders a blood culture which happens to come back positive. He is now about as confident as he'll ever be that his patient has pneumonia.

Of course the culture could have come back negative, which would have surprised the physician, who would then very likely have sent out another specimen. A second negative would then have called for more confirming tests. If these failed, the pneumonia conclusion would have to yield to some of the other rivals and a new line of testing would have to be started.

Having established practical—though never absolute—certainty that Susan has pneumonia, can the doctor possibly be wrong in staying with that conclusion? The catchword here is the term "wrong." The doctor is entirely reasonable and therefore right in the sense that he has chosen as his conclusion the most plausible of the available rivals.

What must not be lost sight of, however, is that in spite of all this—even though he is right in having made his diagnostic decision—it is always, in logical principle, possible—though not probable—for the pneumonia conclusion to be false. Our diagnostic argument is an inductive one and as such its conclusion is never made logically necessary by the premises. Some of the most firmly entrenched inductive conclusions—legal convictions, scientific beliefs, common sense "certainties," etc.—have sometimes had to be rejected with the later discovery of contrary evidence.

And, isn't it (logically) possible, though outrageously preposterous, that Susan faked her symptoms, that she tampered with thermometers, that the physician erred uniformly in his examination, and that the lab people colluded with Susan for some shared hidden purpose? None of these alternative possibilities contradict the premises as they would have if our argument had been a deductive one, that is, if our premises had deductively entailed the pneumonia conclusion.

We reason diagnostically in all sorts of contexts, and on virtually every conceivable level of human inquiry. In daily living we are quick and adept diagnosticians par excellence every step of the way. Here are a few common examples. In each argument, for brevity, only the most plausible conclusion is given and the several premises are joined together as one composite premise. You may find a few of these surprisingly simple and quite ordinary, if not trivial, but they are instances of genuine, moment-to-moment diagnostic reasoning.

> The doorbell is ringing.
>
> Someone's at the door.

The production vice president has asked me to step into his office this morning during coffee break.

Yesterday we had a serious injury in the section I manage.

Ahem—he wants to talk to me about yesterday's accident.

Bill has not heard from his girlfriend for several days now. Last week he forgot to send her a birthday card.

She must be miffed because of his not remembering her birthday.

No one is answering the door.

No one is home.

Smoke!

Fire!

Be careful about distinguishing between the next two examples:

Last night several students on campus separately reported seeing what looked like a bright flying object in the sky.
Therefore
The students did see what looked like a bright flying object in the sky.

Last night several students on campus saw what looked like a bright flying object in the sky.
Therefore
Last night there was, in fact, a bright flying object in the sky.

❋   ❋   ❋

With the help of our examples, we have, so far, been able to make out some rather broad features of diagnostic arguments such as their inductive character (i.e., the conclusion does not necessarily follow from the premises), their innovative (theorizing, hypothesizing) thrust, the rivalry of several possible conclusions, and the stages (we marked off three) over which they can be seen to take shape.

Can we now say something more specific about how the premises of a diagnostic argument relate to its conclusion? Do the premises explain the conclusion, or is it the other way around? What goes into dreaming up an hypothesis? Is there a method to discovery? Finally, how do we actually gauge and compare the relative plausibilities of rival conclusions? Is there any solid criteria that we can go by?

These are the questions for our next chapter.

17

REASONING STRONGLY
AND CREATIVELY:
Diagnosticians We All Are

TWO KINDS OF DIAGNOSTIC PREMISES

For a closer reading of how diagnostic arguments work, it is important to notice that their premises are typically of two very different kinds. One kind describes the presentations (symptoms, appearances, effects, traces) of the scenario before us, e.g., the nose dive at high speed, the cough, the doorbell, the smoke, and so on. The other kind is about the background context, the history, geography, and surrounding circumstances of the event under consideration, for example, the terrain and weather patterns in the area, the pilot's age and flight record, Susan's age and medical history, and so on.

Our conclusion explains the presentations. It is the plunge we make into that deeper reality in order to come up with the causes that explain what confronts us. Thus, the pin-wheel rotor conclusion explains why the aircraft nose-dived; the pneumonia conclusion explains the pain, temperature, and cough; the fire explains the smoke.

On the other hand, a diagnostic conclusion does not explain the background circumstances of an event. Susan's age or her smoking addiction are not explained by the pneumonia conclusion; the pilot's good record or the mountains in the background are not explained by the wind shear conclusion.

Knowing the background circumstances and incorporating this knowledge into our premises, however, helps find the explanation we want. Susan's age, for example, made lung cancer very unlikely, and her upper-middle-class status threw serious doubt on the tuberculosis conclusion. For those with the proper expertise, neighboring mountains could be suggestive of the sort of air turbulence that might throw the tail of an airplane sharply upward to cause a vertical nose dive. And given Susan's heavy smoking, her respiratory symptoms and fever become suggestive of enough chronic inflammation to make her more susceptible to opportunistic lung infection leading to pneumonia. One and the same sort of cough would be suggestive of a chest cold in an otherwise healthy teenager, a tuberculosis infection in a homeless person, and lung cancer in a late-middle-aged suburbanite who has smoked heavily for forty years.

GAUGING OUR GUESSWORK

Okay, given some scenario, any of us can dream up an array of possible conclusions for explaining it. But how do we assess the merit or plausibility of these possible explanations?

THE BACKGROUND OF KNOWLEDGE

Clearly, the knowledge background of the reasoner comes into play in an immediate and very crucial manner. In order to come up with possible causes, we must know a good deal about the world around us, as for example, knowing that anger or annoyance can cause someone to distance herself or that airplanes can be seriously thrown off course by powerful air currents, or that how things look is often a good clue to what they "really" are.

By the time we reach adulthood and probably much before that, we normally accumulate enough background knowledge to make countless diagnostic conjectures possible. What is more, this also enables us to make remarkably good plausibility estimates, based on how good a fit our conjectures make with our background knowledge.

GAUGING BY FREQUENCIES

We can often begin by asking how common, or rare, in terms of what we already know, is the possibility we are considering? Our lung cancer conclusion for Susan describes something which is statistically very rare in a sixteen-year-old. Yes, such a thing does happen. But how often?

And we certainly needn't dip too far into our background knowledge of causes to dismiss outright the possibility that some terrorist magician making incantations in a hidden cave caused the Colorado Springs nose dive. Yes, such a thing is possible in the most general—if you like, "academic" or purely "logical"— sense that, given the facts, it would not be self-contradictory to suppose it. But it is most absurdly improbable, given all we know about the causes that really make things happen in the world.

GAUGING BY EXPLANATORY HURDLES

Most basic of all to the diagnostic process, however, is our sense of the *conclusiveness* of the explanation we are considering. Every one of a set of rival conclusions is an attempt to explain the presentations we are trying to make sense of. It sheds light on the scenario confronting us by singling out possible causes. But how "neat" (conclusive, sufficient) is it?

We have, of course, already seen that, generally speaking, the rival conclusions will not satisfy us equally in this respect. Let's stay with this point a bit longer by going back to some of our examples. The pilot-stroke conclusion to our air disaster argument purports to explain what happened, but such an "explanation" does not conclude the matter. It leaves us with another problem, namely, the task of explaining how a thirty-five-year-old pilot who has consistently registered excellent health can suffer a stroke during the normal maneuvers of landing his aircraft. Would it have been a time-bomb aneurysm deep in his brain first rupturing at that moment? Why had all his physicals failed to detect it? Was it a case of accidental and repeated error in the examination room or did it occur because medical protocols for routine physical examinations do not check for such rare possibilities? What we are facing here is a series of explanatory hurdles that we must address as we try to plug up gaps left in our understanding by the conclusion we are gauging. And, the more hurdles a conclusion poses for us, the lower (in plausibility) we tend to rank it among its rivals.

We seem to have here a solid basis for assessing the relative plausibility of any diagnostic conclusion. Just compare it with its rivals on the basis of the explanatory hurdles it leaves us with. But, what more can we say in support of this kind of strategy?

SIMPLICITY, THE HALLMARK OF TRUTH

In assessing a diagnostic conclusion on the basis of the explanatory hurdles it presents, we are applying a still more fundamental standard—namely, the criterion of simplicity. This is a criterion we are all wedded to in any attempt to make sense of our surroundings. And, quite obviously, the additional conjectures and elaborations we make in vaulting explanatory hurdles will compromise the simplicity of the final account.

Our profound preference for simplicity operates on every level of human inquiry; we all express it constantly in our daily assessments. It is as though we had good reason to believe that reality is never more complex than necessary for explaining its rich and varied appearances.

There is no clearly settled opinion among the students of this subject on how to measure simplicity and on precisely how it counts in the framing and evaluating of hypotheses. Is it merely an aesthetic feature which we favor because it lends elegance and manageability to an hypothesis? Or is it, instead, a logically compelling—perhaps even the ultimate—hallmark of truth?

HOW FIRMLY DO WE HOLD TO OUR BACKGROUND OF BELIEFS?

Let us return now to the role of our background knowledge in our diagnostic search for explanations. Couldn't we always attempt to accommodate or "save" any off-beat conjecture by modifying our background of beliefs about the world instead of modifying the conjecture? In principle, this is always a possibility. Occasionally we do just that—sometimes even in our most "exact" sciences. But we do this rarely. Generally speaking, we owe our loyalty more to our going beliefs than to whatever exotic claims may come along. What is at stake is our overall scientific and common-sense cultures, both of which are intensely reflected in our personal knowledge backgrounds. The established body of basic beliefs we are willing to call knowledge is, in this respect, like the constitution of a stable government. It must be substantially resistant to change, allowing for modification only in the face of very compelling and persistent reasons. To ignore this rule is to threaten the very coherence and stability of our cognitions and of our view of reality. Carried too far, such irreverence can take one to the very edge of sanity.

I am reminded here of a story that was once told me by one of my colleagues:

A despairing young man entered his therapist's office morbidly insisting that he (the young man) was dead. The therapist, taken aback, tried to calm her visitor with assurances that he was very much alive. When it became apparent that ordinary measures wouldn't work, she promised some "proof" and pricked him with a needle.

"There," she said, "you're quite alive; you're bleeding!"

"No," muttered the young man, "that only proves that corpses bleed!"

REASONABLENESS

In discussing the plausibility of diagnostic arguments, we have, so far, been concerned basically with assessing the relative plausibilities of rival conclusions so we can rank them. Our purpose in ranking them obviously has to do with choosing the best conclusion for our diagnostic argument.

This purpose can be made clearer, however, by noting that it is twofold. First of all, we want our final argument to be the reasonable one. This means that the conclusion we choose for it is the most plausible of the available rivals. Obviously, if we absolutely had to bet on any one of our rival conclusions, we would of course want to bet on the most plausible one, no matter how weak its supporting argument was. Secondly, we want to be able to say something about how strong our final argument actually is. And here we must be cautious; even when an argument is reasonable it may still be weak. This, as we have already noted, will happen when the plausibility of our conclusion is not much greater than the combined plausibilities of its rivals.

To see this, recall for a moment our early diagnostic reasoning about the Colorado Springs air disaster. There, for the sake of discussion, we assigned 45 percent, 35 percent, and 20 percent to the wind shear, locked controls, and stroke conclusions, respectively. On this assignment, the reasonable conclusion would clearly be the most plausible one, namely, the wind shear conclusion.

Although this was the most plausible conclusion, it was also more likely to be false than true. The reason for this was that its plausibility was 45 percent. And this is less than 55 percent, the remaining plausibility of the other two (alternative) conclusions combined, i.e., stroke or jammed controls. Yes, paradoxically enough, it is more likely that the cause of the crash was either jammed controls or a stroke than that it was the wind.

Note as well, that if we could have assigned a 55 percent plausibility to the wind shear conclusion, it would then, of course, have come out more likely to be true than false.

WIDENING THE PLAUSIBILITY GAP

Even so, the resulting argument would still have been very weak, for the odds would be only 5 percent above even—hardly a winning bet above its rivals combined. The strength of a diagnostic argument, therefore, depends upon how far the plausibility of its conclusion stands above that of its rivals combined.

Calling this difference a *plausibility gap,* we can now say that the greater this plausibility gap, the greater the strength of the argument. Clearly, a conclusion which greatly outranks its rivals combined is the conclusion of a strong argument. Only then will it get the lion's share of the total available plausibility (100 percent) among all rivals.

It now becomes apparent that when the second and third stages of our diagnostic reasoning strengthen our diagnostic arguments, they do so by widening the plausibility gap between the most plausible conclusion and its rivals combined. This happens as the additional evidence which is produced favors the conclusion more and more over its rivals. Finally, the third or confirmation stage, if positive, increases this gap decisively, to yield practical, though never absolute, certainty.

DIAGNOSTIC REASONING AS A CREATIVE LEAP

How do we ever manage to dream up rival conclusions in the first place? Is there some kind of recipe for doing so—something like "a logic of discovery"?

It would be great to have such a thing, but logicians have never formulated one. Does this mean, therefore, that the first cognitive step in diagnostic reasoning—the leap that generates possible hypotheses—is an intuitive flash which cannot be reduced to anything else? Is it an act of miraculous creativity, a *sturm und drang* insight beyond all logical scrutiny and for which there are no teachable strategies?

Many writers from antiquity to modern times have urged that it is no more than just that: an inspiration which cannot be further analyzed or understood in terms of any other form of cognition. Despite the high authority of some of those who have backed this view, it remains undeniable that a vast proportion of all our diagnostic inferences are not all that occult. Yes, we smell smoke and instantly cry "Fire!" The paramedic at the scene of an accident feels a pulse and quickly mutters, "Still alive." Our ability to do this sort of thinking is certainly uncanny. But a moment's reflection reveals much about how we actually do it.

The major portion of the diagnostic inferences which we make throughout our lives are made in the most familiar situations. In these contexts, the relevant connections between causes and effects are firmly established associations made on the basis of personal experiences strengthened by everything else we have learned from teachers, books, friends, the media, and so on.

Diagnostic reasoning goes "backward," as it were, from effects to causes. And it is no great trick to dip into this background and come up quickly—sometimes almost instantly—with some explanation of what confronts us. Most remarkably, when we do this we often come up with even more than this. We entertain not merely one, but several competing possibilities (rival conclusions). We usually feel most confident about one of them. And to top it all, we even sense how much strength to allot our reasoning.

In the more specialized contexts like plane crashes, health care, crime mysteries, etc., diagnostic thinking is basically no different. In such contexts, it is the experts who usually do most of the thinking. But here too, as in ordinary contexts, the inferences proceed "backward," as it were, from observed effects or symptoms to possible causes. Only this time, the specialized background knowledge of the expert is what guides her reasoning.

So, it is possible and, perhaps, more enlightening, to regard this "flash" explanatory thinking in both ordinary and more specialized contexts, as essentially a case of very fast diagnostic reasoning, rather than as some kind of irreducible intuition. Viewed in this manner, the key to the reasoning agility we have is seen not as miraculous "inspiration" but as strong familiarity with the kinds of objects and events involved and with the underlying causes that move them.

Everything we know about human thinking says that intimate acquaintance with the subject matter is indispensable for perceiving possible connections. Every relevant association, no matter how minor or tangential, is operative in guiding us to the mark. Without a doubt, the more we know about the causal relations within the subject-matter under consideration, the more successfully and rapidly we reason diagnostically about it. Generally speaking, "Leave some of it to the experts" is profoundly sound advice.

THE PLUNGE TO A DEEPER UNDERWORLD

There is, however, a very special kind of diagnostic thinking which we have had to keep out of consideration so far because of its extraordinary character. This is the kind of thinking that scientists engage in when they propose novel theories in order to explain what we experience with our senses. It is no doubt in connection with this kind of thinking that the "pure inspiration" claim about diagnostic thinking gathers most of its force. According to these claims we simply "see" a new concept—a new theory—we do not get to it as the conclusion of an argument.

Okay, then: Let's see what's so very special about the reasoning that goes into scientific theorizing.

SCIENTIFIC WORLDMAKING:
The Ultimate Diagnostic Leap

> Believing as I do in the regularity of nature I cannot stop abruptly where our microscopes cease to be of use. Here the vision of the mind authoritatively supplements the vision of the eye.
>
> John Tyndall

Typically, scientific theory gives a causal account or explanation of our sense experiences in terms of intangible things like atoms, electrons, microwaves, and so on. Science has collected a considerable assortment of such "hypothetical" entities, all of them either too small or too abstract to be observed directly with any of our senses.

Still the theoretician regards these so-called unobservables as (real) causes of virtually everything she sees, hears, tastes, touches, or otherwise observes in the sensible world. That is, she thinks diagnostically about the phenomena she experiences. She draws her conclusions (hypotheses), however, not in terms of tangible wind currents, visible lung congestions, or concrete weight gains. Instead she frames them in terms of entities which she has never experienced and—in the case of nearly all such entities—can never experience. Science describes the visible in terms of the invisible—even the "permanently invisible."

The contrast here with ordinary diagnostic reasoning is radical. In ordinary diagnostic reasoning we go from observable effects to observable causes on the basis of having already associated these through experience. In scientific theorizing we reason diagnostically from observable effects to hidden causes and therefore not on the basis of having already associated both through sense experience.

Well then, how do we come up with such causes, causes of a kind we have never seen or touched before? Is this simply the magic play of a wildly fantasizing, inscrutable imagination, or is there some "logic" or method in it—some set of strategies which, if known and followed, could to some extent enhance the scientist's ability to theorize or, at least, help us understand the process?

How, for example, did the ancient Greeks more than two thousand years ago come up with the fabulous idea that all of physical reality is made up of tiny particles too small to be seen by anyone, too hard to be divided, and too restless to stop bouncing around in empty space? Was this vision of matter just inexplicable inspiration, or could it be viewed as a case of diagnostic reasoning—the process we've been examining?

Although the first writings on this wonderful theory are nearly all lost, we have good reason to believe that its authors were trying to make sense of the familiar fact that different substances generally have different densities. Water was obviously less dense than lead and more dense than steam. No doubt, these ancients had the required familiarity with the subject matter involved. Stones, sand, air, water, metals, and so on must have been subjects of real interest to them.

Some philosophers, led by Parmenedes of Elea, in their passion for simplicity, had been saying that matter is all basically of one unchangeable kind and that diversity manifests itself only on the level of appearances rather than on the deeper levels of reality. To explain change and, in particular, variations in density therefore, Democritus concluded that objects were a "mix" of space and one and the same kind of (Parmenedean) matter.

This of course required particles. For, if basic matter was all the same, and hence all of the same density, the only way of mixing it with space was to imagine that tangible objects were constructed of discrete particles with spaces between them. The wider the spaces, the less the overall density of the matter!

It all seemed fine for objects that were visibly granular or porous. Sandstone was less dense than granite and pumice was almost light enough to float. But lead and iron were not granular at all. They were obviously smoothly solid, malleable, ductile, continuous—rather than discrete—substances.

Still, iron was considerably less dense than lead. The answer was not all that hard to give. Just imagine the particles constituting any visibly grainy object to be shrinking. As they get smaller and smaller the object as a whole will look less and less grainy. After a certain point in the process, the constituent particles will no longer be individually visible, and the object will look as smoothly solid as does the metal of any sword or wine cup.

All that Democritus needed, now, was a force of attraction between his atoms. For even while they continued to bounce so as to maintain some "average space" between themselves, this force would keep them close enough together to form a visibly solid object. Again, the restless atoms as well as the spaces between them were so small that the granularity of the object could never be detected by any human eye.

This simple example of diagnostic reasoning in early science, i.e., Greek atomic theory, illustrates some rather neat thinking, largely moved along by at least two key (logical) strategies.

The first of these is the criterion of simplicity which we have already discussed as a basis for gauging the plausibility of a diagnostic conclusion. First of all, the theory supposes "basic" matter to be all of one kind, or at least of one density. Secondly, it rejects the alternative to atomism, namely that matter can be continuously subdivided without end. Limitless or infinite processes of this sort have been notoriously mind-boggling enigmas in the history of human thought. Democritus, one of the authors of the atomic theory, must surely have wanted to avoid this complication. Besides, he had no need of infinite divisibility. Once atoms were conceived as small enough to be forever invisible they could remain acceptably finite and still explain all they were required to explain, so why bother with further subdivision?

The second strategy at work in our example is the use of analogy, a form of reasoning we have already discussed. In reasoning from visible to invisible graininess the atomists drew analogies. Starting from the fact that the density of a visibly grainy object depends on how big the average spaces are between its component particles, they went to a similar dependency at the invisible level.

At any rate, the question of how much discernable systematic method and how much sheer "revelation" or irreducible insight goes into the kind of diagnostic thinking that leads to a theoretical breakthrough is an issue with which we need not seriously tangle here. Our example, however, strongly suggests that definable strategies can substantially guide such thinking, even when it involves inventing new and "unobservable" subject matter.

True, the history of science is studded with instances in which theoretical ideas have come to their authors in a flash or dream and, as it seems, outside the pale of any explicitly articulated process. Superbly spontaneous though this sort of thinking is, it may still be useful to see it as closely tied to genuine reasoning rather than to pure revelation. The high speed with which theoretical insights sometimes come to their authors could obscure the subtly systematic and strategic aspects of the thinking, but they do not negate it. At any rate, one thing is for sure. The very moment we begin to evaluate and confirm or disconfirm our hypotheses—no matter how they appear to first bubble up in us—we are squarely involved in the diagnostic reasoning process.

✳   ✳   ✳

This completes our discussion of diagnostic reasoning in its most general features. We've characterized it as the most creative, richly productive kind of inductive reasoning. In our next chapter, I would like to touch briefly on an enormously important kind of reasoning rarely recognized in the literature as being ultimately a special kind of diagnostic reasoning. I am referring here to *statistical reasoning*.

The methods of statistics have become very formal and systematic, and therefore are less creatively inspired than the kind of conjectural, diagnostic thinking we pull off in "flash framing" a hypothesis. But, by the same token, statistics, with its powerful mathematical paraphernalia, is a logical resource so central in modern life that no field of endeavor can successfully ignore it.

The arcane technical details of this subject are far beyond our purposes here, but a light touch on a few key aspects will serve two purposes: It will point up the fundamentally diagnostic basis of statistical reasoning, and it will alert us to some of the errors we all tend to commit as we wade through the flood of statistical information that engulfs us virtually every moment of our daily existence. These errors are so common that they could well be considered statistical fallacies, deserving of full membership among the standard fallacies we discussed in part two.

18

STATISTICS, MUDDLES, AND GENERALIZATIONS:
Slippery Stuff!

UNIVERSAL GENERALIZATION

Superficially similar to, but importantly different from, simple prediction, which was detailed in chapter 15, is *universal generalization*—often more simply referred to as *generalization*. When we generalize, we reason from a set of particular instances to some general (universal) claim:

> All metals are electrical conductors.

> All humans are mortal.

An example of the argument involved would be:

As observed so far, all organisms with a spine have had hearts.
Therefore (Probably)
All organisms with spines have hearts.

This kind of argument is of course inductive. It is clearly possible, though perhaps improbable, that the conclusion is false despite the true premises. We may simply have not yet found the possibly existing exceptions, namely, organisms that have spines but no hearts.

Generalization and simple prediction are easily confused. The two kinds of inference resemble each other because in both, the more cases the premises refer to, the stronger the argument. Recall that the greater the number of lemons we tasted, all of which were sour, the more support there was for the conclusion that the very next one would be sour.

The resemblance, however, ends there. Unlike simple prediction, the conclusion of a generalization describes an entire population, rather than merely the very next case. Recall our example ending with the sourness of the next lemon? The following example is different:

> All the lemons I've ever tasted have been sour.
> *Therefore (Probably)*
> All lemons are sour.

Notice that the conclusion is about the entire population of lemons. Notice also that it serves to explain the observations which led to it. Obviously, the circumstance of all lemons being sour would solidly explain why the ones I've tasted are. Our argument, therefore, is diagnostic. It concludes with an hypothesis about the underlying reality that accounts for the observations we've actually made. And this, of course, is not so in simple prediction. The next lemon's being sour (conclusion) does not in the least explain why all the others have been (premises).

BOLSTERING OUR GENERALIZATIONS:
Confirmation

Once we have made a generalization from a number of particular instances, we may later encounter new, "confirming" instances of it. These are confirmations in the sense that they strengthen our generalization (diagnostic conclusion) because they are, in effect, an addition to the supporting instances we had in the first place.

It is, of course, critically important that generalizations *not* be made on evidence that is too scanty to begin with. Yet, despite the obviousness of this caveat, we are all inveterate generalizers, and easily fall into the error of doing it too hastily. Generalizing to the conclusion that all lemons are sour yields us a falsehood. Not all lemons are. For most of us this is an excusable result; few of us have ever encountered a sweet lemon, even over a lifetime of lemons.

Some universal generalizations, however, are much weaker and far less excusable. I'll never forget the shocking experience I had when I tasted what must have been the fourth or fifth persimmon I had ever encountered. The first few I had eaten at the home of a persimmon enthusiast over several visits. On every occasion, the large orange fruit was incomparably delicious— delicately flavored, honey-sweet, and smooth of texture. My conclusion: All orange persimmons are incomparably delicious.

I finally got around to buying some that looked very much like the ones I had enjoyed, and offered them to our guests as an after-dinner treat, urging them to "Just bite and enjoy!"

What followed could have been a sit-com scenario. They (and I along with them) scampered desperately for liquids—speechless in the grip of an unimaginable mouth-puckering and tongue-curling experience. I should have had much more mouth-to-fruit contact with persimmons before generalizing, and more background knowledge would have helped refine my observations. Though seemingly okay by their general color, the persimmons were not fully ripe and therefore totally inedible, Persimmons must be very soft and a touch deeper in color to be palatable.

STATISTICAL GENERALIZATION

Statistics is a subtle and complex branch of applied mathematics, useful in basically two ways: (1) It furnishes synoptic overviews of large quantities of numerical data in terms of averages, distributions, correlations, percentages, and more; (2) It deals with how to arrive at a conclusion about some population, by examining not the entire population, but instead, a relatively small sample from that population.

> I scooped up some nuts from that supermarket bin, and out of fifteen, five of them were almonds.
> *Therefore (Probably)*
> The nut mixture in the bin is (about) one-third almonds.

This process is called *statistical generalization*. It is, we might say, a more general form of inference than universal generalization. Whereas in universal generalization we go from a uniform experience (all my past lemons have been sour) to a universal conclusion (all lemons are sour), in statistical generalization we go from a "mixed" experience (five out of fifteen nuts were almonds) to a statistical conclusion, usually expressed in percentages, anywhere from 0 to 100 percent, inclusively.

Reasoning from sample to population is one of the most natural and genial of all forms of inference. We do it all the time and in every conceivable type of situation. Therefore we never ask how it works—a matter not quite obvious. So let's pause for a few words about this hugely important and fundamental mode of reasoning.

In our daily affairs, statistical reasoning is typically casual. The sampling is crude and the numbers only approximate. The process, however, remains essentially systematic and numerical, leaving little room for the kind of conjectural and hypothetical thinking that we have been calling diagnostic. Still, it is diagnostic reasoning nonetheless. It is diagnostic because it yields a conclusion that explains a set of findings.

Let me pause on this a bit longer. Our purpose in sampling a population is to be able to say something plausible about the parent population. To do this we draw a sample from the population, and make what we discover about the sample our premises. Our conclusion is then about the population, and it is the one that best explains our findings about the sample.

To see that this is so, we must fall back on a basic statistical principle which, unfortunately, is hardly ever mentioned in books on statistics. This is the fact that the *most probable* proportions (percentages) in a randomly drawn sample are the same proportions that exist in the population. This is a fact of statistical theory which we cannot digress to demonstrate here, but whose proof is mathematically quite straightforward. It is this deeply fundamental fact which justifies our ascribing to the whole population the statistical properties of the sample.

As in all inductive reasoning, what statistical arguments provide is *probability,* and probability is the guide of life. Used properly, therefore, statistical reasoning can give us a sharp edge over the flukes of blind chance. But in the hands of the unwary or the dishonest, the subtleties of statistics can make it the most slippery game in town. Even as nonexperts, however, we can go a long way toward guarding against bad statistical reasoning by learning to recognize some of the most commonly committed forms of it.

Here are what I believe to be the five most common types of statistical pitfalls, all of them exceedingly risky. Let's call them *statistical fallacies.* May I add that, because of the somewhat abstract and quantitative element in these fallacies, they are, compared to the standard fallacies that we've already discussed, probably the trickiest of all to detect.

STATISTICAL FALLACIES

THE BIASED SAMPLE: A Disaster Waiting to Happen

Basically, a statistical inference from some sample attempts to say whether a given population or large set of things probably has some interesting statistical property (P). The inference may, for example, tell us that a certain percentage of a population is

HIV-positive. Obviously, for such an inference to work the sample must be fair, that is, representative of the population. This means that it must be drawn in a way that does not favor or disfavor the occurrence of P.

For example, trying to determine the extent of affluence in a given American town by using as a sample the cars parked in one of its major supermarkets on a day in August will not do. The more affluent townspeople may be on vacation during that month. Also, the most affluent do not generally shop in supermarkets. A less risky sampling procedure would be to go to a telephone directory, obtain the addresses on every tenth page of the directory, and then go see the residences corresponding to these addresses. But even this more neutral strategy may not be entirely free of bias. It may indeed be the case that comparatively many of the most prosperous residents do not list in telephone books. A still more neutral approach might be that of going to the income tax returns. Only those returns would be examined with social security numbers ending in, say, a two or a six—assuming of course that such records were legally accessible.

Selecting representative samples is a difficult and critical affair requiring full use of our background knowledge. Failure to draw a fair sample can lead to disastrously misleading results. A celebrated example which authors on this subject never tire of mentioning is the demise of the *Literary Digest* after it predicted in 1936 that the Republican presidential nominee, Alf Landon, would defeat the Democratic incumbent, Franklin Roosevelt, by a landslide. To the utter embarrassment of the *Digest*, it was Roosevelt instead who won by a landslide. The *Digest* folded soon after. This example is worth repeating because it so dramatically illustrates the fallacy of the biased sample—in this case committed by those who, one would think, should have known better.

Middle and working class Americans, vastly outnumbering the affluent, had been hit hard by the Great Depression, unemployment and poverty among them reaching pandemic proportions. The sweeping labor union movements of the 1920s made Democrats of most workers, and many of them subscribed to the widespread belief that former President Herbert Hoover and his Republican party had caused the hard times. The *Digest* polled voters by phone, not remembering that (in those days) only the more affluent voters, who tended to be Republicans, had telephones!

THE UNDERSIZED SAMPLE: Too Little to Go By

Obviously when a sample is known to be completely representative as, for example, a few drops from a gallon of homogeneous wine, the sample can be as small as conveniently possible. More typically, however, there is some uncertainty about how representative any given sample might be. In such a case, the larger the sample, the more reliable it is. It can be demonstrated mathematically (and we cannot take this detour here) that as the sample is made larger, there are more ways in which it can come up with the same statistical properties as the parent population. That is, as the sample increases in size, the probability that it will differ statistically from the population from which it was drawn drops off significantly. Another way of putting this is to say that the plausibility gap between attributing to the population the same statistical properties as the sample and doing otherwise, widens—the likelihood that our conclusion is the correct one increases—as the sample is made larger. So, the larger the sample, the more likely it is to be representative.

We don't have to be mathematical statisticians to get a sense of this; we can easily see that tiny samples constitute very weak evidence. The percentages in the composition of a very small sample can easily be statistical flukes that fluctuate wildly by adding just one or two individuals to the sample. For example, if we draw a sample of only one marble from a bag of red and white ones, it will come out either 100 percent red ones or 0 percent red ones regardless of the composition the entire collection. If we draw a sample of two marbles the possible percentages of red marbles become 100 percent, 50 percent, and 0 percent, and so on. Clearly, the samples must be larger before we begin to get some stable, significant data. Even more obvious is the other extreme, in which the sample is the entire population. In that trivial case, the sample, of course, has precisely the same statistical properties as the population, so that the inference from sample to population becomes a certainty. Obviously, considerations of economy and convenience place practical limits on how large we can make any sample.

CONFUSED POPULATIONS:
A Deep and Frequent Muddle

In a recent polemic against the charge that our system of justice has been racially biased, one distinguished speaker reported that throughout this century more whites have been convicted of a capital offense than blacks. The intent of this remark seems to have been that of suggesting that the system is no more likely to convict a black defendant than it is a white one. What the speaker did not say, however, is that there are more whites in our population than there are blacks.

To illustrate this fallacy more concretely, let us start with a more specific example. Suppose we have a representative sample of all the men in this country who test HIV-positive and find 75 percent of them married (and of course, 25 percent unmarried). Can we take this as an indication that, in general, married men are a higher risk group for HIV than unmarried ones? Decidedly not? If we do, we are confusing populations. To get the higher-risk group we want to compare two populations, namely, married men and unmarried men. We must do it by comparing the percentage of HIV carriers in each of these groups, not the percentage of each of these groups among all men with HIV. All we can properly infer from our data is that about 75 percent of all men with HIV are married.

Still, given this statistic, it is very tempting to conclude hastily that married males are the higher risk group. To highlight the fallacy in such an inference, imagine the following make-believe numbers:

Suppose that the total population of men is 100 million and that 80 million or 80 percent of them are married. Now suppose that 0.075 percent of the married men are HIV positive, and that 0.1 percent of the unmarried ones are HIV positive. Clearly, then, comparing these last two populations, unmarried men are at about 33 percent more risk than married men, because 0.1 is about 33 percent larger than .075. But the number of married men who are HIV-positive is .075 percent of 80 million, or 60,000. The number of unmarried men who are HIV positive is 0.1 percent of 20 million or 20,000. This means that in the total of 80,000 men with HIV, 60,000 or 75 percent are married and 20,000 or 25 percent are not. Naturally, therefore, in a representative sample of adult males with HIV, 75 percent would be married and only 25 percent not—despite the fact that unmarried men are at substantially greater risk than married ones!

The air of paradox disappears once we realize that comparing the percentages of married to unmarried among those with HIV is wrong because these numbers do not depend only on the percentage of HIV carriers in each group. They depend also on the relative sizes of the two populations being compared, namely, the total of married men and the total of unmarried men.

MISLEADING PERCENTAGES: Careful Attention!

How about the announcement that the rate of violent crimes in a certain city has doubled in the past year? What may not have been noted is that the year before, just two violent crimes were committed making this past year's tally only four, still very low and no cause for alarm. When considering such percentage increases, it is, for most purposes, important to be aware also of the absolute numerical amounts involved.

Other examples:

There are only 25 parts per million (0.0025 percent) of lead in some drinking water.

Yet this tiny percentage, 0.0025 percent, may be a serious health hazard (it may cause mental retardation, etc.) to growing children. The allowable, so-called action ratio, is 15 parts per million or only 0.0015 percent.

85 percent of what is in your milk container is water.

But all you need is the other 15 percent for palatable "whole" milk.

90 percent of you is only water, and the rest not worth much in chemicals.

It better be that way or else! This quip says nothing about the complex and critical way in which it is all organized to form a living being.

This year, the rate of increase in the incidence of tuberculosis has quadrupled over last year.

This does not mean that there were four times more reported cases this year than last year. It means that, for example, if last year there were, say, 1,001 cases, as compared to 1,000 the year before, this year there were 1,005 cases—vastly different from 4,004 cases! Remember, what is being measured is the *rate of increase*. Last year there was an increase of one case over the year before (1,001, up from 1,000). Four times this increase of one case is four cases, bringing this year's total to 1,005.

The fallacy in all of these consists in our being misled by the percentages either because the absolute quantities are more important or because we are not paying proper attention to what the percentages are measuring.

REFERENCE CLASS MAKES A DIFFERENCE

A *reference class* fallacy is committed when we apply statistical generalizations to an individual without being careful about which groups we are referring him to. An individual may simultaneously be a member of many classes. He may, for example, be under twenty-five, single, a smoker, a nondrinker, a city dweller, short-tempered, and so on, and therefore simultaneously belong to all of these groups. Obviously, in attempting to gauge the likelihood of a certain thing happening to him we would have to take into account his membership in some of these groups. The question is, "Which ones?" The answer is, "All the relevant ones." And we must rely on our background knowledge to decide which these are. One of the problems with doing this is that the number of relevant groups may be indefinite.

Imagine, for example, a small start-up insurance firm in some developing country trying to assign an auto accident insurance premium to an applicant driver. It has no established protocols for assigning premiums but has access to accident statistics for various groups of drivers in that country. The only restrictions are that the rates must be both competitive and profitable.

To accomplish this task, the statistician of the company must take into account the likelihood that the applicant driver will have a serious accident during the coming year. The driver is a licensed male, and, if the statistician had no other information about him, she would have to judge him on the basis of the frequencies, in percentages, of serious accidents among members of that reference class, namely, the class of all licensed male drivers in that country.

She knows, however, that he is also over twenty-five—which now changes the reference class to male driver over twenty-five. The accident frequency and therefore the likelihood of a serious accident is relatively lower for this group. She also learns that he has driven for six years and done so safely. The new reference class is now male driver over twenty-five with no accidents for six years. In addition, he is a nondrinker, married, with children, and will do nearly all his driving in a suburban setting. She obtains statistics for each resulting reference class as it narrows with every new characteristic and finds the accident frequencies and therefore the likelihoods changing significantly at each step.

Had the broker stopped narrowing down her reference class anywhere along the way, she would have come up with a different likelihood each time. What should she do? The reasonable thing to do, clearly, would be to narrow down the reference class as much as is relevantly and practically possible and as much as her available statistics will allow. She of course knows that some characteristics like eye color, height, weight, and food preferences are not relevant. She therefore does not seek any statistics for reference classes further narrowed by such traits.

The broker commits a statistical fallacy if, in her decisions, she fails to take reference class into account. She must recognize that the likelihoods she comes up with are critically dependent on how she has narrowed that reference class.

For a simpler example, consider a nutritionist who wants her patient, Slim, to gain weight. Slim loves spices, particularly pepper. Imagine now that she does a limited survey of the literature and finds that certain spices like red and black pepper tend to lower food consumption. In light of this information, she advises Slim to stay away from pepper. Later, however, she imagines that those who have an unusually strong liking for pepper may actually eat *more* with it, so back she goes to search further.

Quite remarkably, she finds a study saying that, though for the general population spices tend to decrease food consumption, those who have an unusually strong love of spices tend to eat considerably more when they use them. This of course completely reverses the likelihoods and therefore her advice to Slim.

*   *   *

So far we have discussed both good and bad reasoning and in particular, the structures of deductive and inductive arguments. Our examples have been entirely about concrete things of the world: lost wallets, burglaries, inflation, illness, and so on. These are the things we most often reason about.

Sometimes, however, even in our most mundane daily

affairs, we find ourselves grappling with much more abstract subject matter: an idea, a meaning, a concept. We tangle with such intangibles when we want to analyze and clarify some fuzzy idea, and, more rarely, when we try to come up with or synthesize a brand new one. Besides being very enlightening and therefore fulfilling, this kind of activity is central to reflective thinking at every level of discourse. Let us go, then, to our next chapter where we'll do some concept surgery, and so engage in the art of analyzing, synthesizing, and differentiating ideas.

Part Four

IDEAS:
Concept Surgery

19

ANALYTICAL THINKING:
Unpacking a Familiar Idea

Rationalism is an adventure in the clarification of thought.
Alfred North Whitehead (1861–1947)

THINKING ANALYTICALLY

Language consists of words and their meanings along with some rules or conventions (written or not) that are generally observed for using these items. It is a mighty tool—the prosthesis that amplifies our intelligence a limitless amount and infuses this intelligence into our surroundings. It is no doubt the one thing that most heralds our Darwinian passage from intelligent ape-hood to creative human-hood. Words and their shadows, i.e., concepts or meanings, are what we work on in lining up and honing this marvelous tool. Let's look into the process to see how some of this happens.

When did you and a few friends last sit in a circle after a provoking movie or play and ask, What is friendship, justice, liberty, love, beauty, happiness, or any other countless concepts? When you did anything like this, you very likely got swept into the intriguing and entangling process of analyzing (dissecting or unpacking) an idea.

Throughout this discussion, the terms "concept," "idea," "notion," and "meaning" are all interchangeable. I personally prefer the terms "concept" and "idea," but the other terms will, from time to time, inevitably make their way into our discussion.

Actually, the concept of 'friendship' did come up one evening when, in connection with a film we had just seen, someone asked, "What is it to be a friend?" "Defining" an everyday concept as familiar as this one seemed at first to be a straightforward, if not idle, affair. After all we certainly "knew" what friendship was. The rest would be simply a matter of recalling one or two of the best friendships any of us had ever had and then, on the basis of these, giving a thumbnail sketch of the relationship. But we found that our thumbnail sketches were okay only for a start. No sooner did we give one than it seemed to be in need of some sort of revision.

We might of course have gone to a good dictionary or even a philosophical essay on friendship to help settle the matter. On this occasion, however, our aim was something quite different. We wanted to make sense of a concept with which we were already entirely acquainted and generally knew how to apply in ordinary situations, but which we had never tried to define and sharpen for ourselves. What we were trying to do is analyze the idea of friendship.

Someone kicked off the discussion by suggesting that friendship is a relationship in which the parties seek and enjoy each other's company and welfare, and in which there is affection or esteem for each other. No sooner was this said than there were some second thoughts. We recalled that we had held some of our teachers in very high esteem, wanted the best for them, and even enjoyed their company—and also that the feelings had to some extent been mutual. Yet we could not really say that they had been friends of ours. Our start-up "definition," therefore, seemed to need revision to include something about commitment, loyalty, and possibly even about how long the individuals had known each other. Also, close relatives, spouses, and lovers might each have to be figured in somehow. The term "friend," used without careful qualification, could be seriously misleading for some of these relationships. But the time was too short that evening to conclude the matter to anybody's satisfaction.

Would the discussion have been more manageable if the topic had been another one, say, justice, instead of friendship? One of us might have ventured a "definition" like this:

> Justice is what we have when we give individuals their due of both good and bad things—money, goods, privileges, freedoms, rewards, punishments, and so on.

How helpful would this definition have been? Does it tell us how to decide what is due whom? If "what is due someone" means nothing other than "what is justly owed that individual," are we not back to square one; aren't we begging the question of what is justice? To break the circle we would want to say, more explicitly, how one decides who gets what. Would we give or take from individuals according to their needs, abilities, wealth, efforts, productivity, age, heritage, or other criteria?

What about the case of deserved punishment in punitive or criminal justice? How does retribution fit in with correction and rehabilitation? Is there any place for vengeance? We see once again that without more thought, our analysis risks being either circular or uselessly shallow and incomplete.

ANALYZING A CONCEPT

It certainly looks like analyzing a concept is a kind of reasoning—one that can be rather complex. Like all reasoning, it involves deliberation and also takes us from "old" to "new" insights—a transition that reminds us of the move from premises to conclusions. Okay then, what more can we say about it? If it is reasoning, what kind of reasoning is it?

As one dictionary definition has it, the term "analysis" refers loosely to any detailed study for the purpose of understanding something complex—a literary work, a system of things, a situation, and so on. What we want, however, is a more specific sense of the term, one that conveys the notion of uncovering or "opening up" a concept. The sense we have in mind is analogous to what an analytical chemist does in order to determine the composition of some unknown substance. He divides it by chemical and physical means into the parts that constitute it.

Similarly, when we say we are engaged in analytical thinking we mean that we try to "dissect" a more or less complex concept that we're already familiar with and already know how to use. We unpack the concept so as to get at its parts—its components concepts. This, then, provides an explicit basis for how we, in actual practice, use the concept. In this sense, it supplements or "fills out" our understanding of it.

To help illustrate the process, let us go to a fresh example. This time, let's see if we can do something in the way of unpacking the concept of 'liberty' in the societal sense of the term.

Long and famous essays have been written on liberty. It is a familiar concept which lies deep in the American tradition and pops up constantly. Developing an extended discussion of liberty is certainly beyond our purposes here. What we can do is show the direction which an analysis of the idea might take.

Okay, let's start by noting how our term, "liberty," is ordinarily used. Which are some of the societies that we would say have liberty—societies we would call "free"? Actually we need focus on only one of these, a representative one. We can then use this instance of liberty as a model and examine it for the characteristics that we're looking for. The reliability of our choice of representative case is assured by the fact that we have a full acquaintance and recognition (what philosophers call knowledge by acquaintance) of the concept we're analyzing.

Concrete representative examples of this sort are powerful tools in any analysis of abstract concepts. Analytical philosophers call them paradigm cases. Their concreteness makes it easy to "read off" features or "components" of the concept we want to dissect. The paradigm case which easily comes to mind for liberty is of course contemporary American democracy—though almost any other industrialized democracy would also do for a start. At any rate, our paradigm suggests majority rule or government by the people (*demos* = people, *kratos* = power) as a major characteristic of a free society.

This feature alone as a full characterization of a free society would soon run us aground. Our deeper sense of the term "liberty" raises a red flag. Majority rule, though apparently essential to democracy, could not possibly be enough. The majority can tyrannize the minority: What about the "rights" of the individual or of any relatively small group? How are they to be defined and secured in the context of the whole? In this connection, we easily recall a glaring counterexample, namely, America of less than 150 years ago in which majority rule permitted mass repression and coercion in the form of human slavery.

Notice how a counterexample works and what a powerful knockdown weapon it is. In our example, it satisfies the preliminary, thumbnail characterization of liberty as majority rule—but it does intolerable violence to what we understand by 'liberty.' Or, what comes to the same thing, it clashes uncomfortably with how we ordinarily use the term "liberty." Why? A counterexample essentially presents an explanatory hurdle which undermines the plausibility of the analysis to whatever point we've taken it so far. How, for example do we explain slavery in a free society?

Our initial account of liberty, therefore, needs repairing, so let's take a second look at our paradigm case. Doing this tells us that the liberty contemporary Americans enjoy consists of much more than the power to elect government. It also includes such essential freedoms as freedom from certain coercions like loss of privacy, unwarranted arrest, and torture to force betrayal.

Would these freedoms, together with majority rule, suffice to define liberty? Can we imagine a society that has these blessings but that would serve as a counterexample to even this result of our analysis?

Okay, it's time for still another look at our paradigm case which again suggests that more goes into the making of a free society. We would also want to include certain positive freedoms, more specifically, the freedoms to engage in those activities that are clearly necessary for the pursuit of happiness and personal fulfillment. We might have in mind, here, such activities as assembling in groups, speaking one's mind, participating fully in the political process, engaging in commerce, obtaining a formal education, and having children. The required freedoms, then, are of at least two sorts—freedoms *from* and freedoms *to* or empowerments.

Our conceptual analysis could go on to further refinements, so that 'liberty,' in the socio-political sense in which we have considered it here, turns out to be no simple idea.

WHAT KIND OF REASONING IS CONCEPT ANALYSIS?

What can we say about the thinking that our examples illustrated? One thing is for sure, it was reasoning, all right. But of what kind? The tentativeness, uncertainty, and revisions on the basis of evidence point to induction. Furthermore, the on-going references to the phenomenon of usage—along with the complexities and the creative conjecture they called for—are strongly suggestive of a diagnostic process.

Recall that in diagnostic reasoning, there is a scenario—a set of traces or presentations—and a conclusion that explains the scenario. In our examples, say, the one about liberty, the scenario was not some concrete happening like a plane crash, a crime scene, or a set of medical symptoms, but something far less tangible. What we were looking at was what we generally "understand" by the concept of 'liberty,' or—what is essentially equivalent to this—the manner in which we apply this concept to actual or possible societies. This, in turn, amounts to nothing other than how we ordinarily use the term "liberty."

The conclusion of our reasoning, which explicitly specified what liberty consists of, was an attempt to explain this scenario. It gave the underlying conceptual content, the "conceptual reality," as it were, behind our familiarity or acquaintance with (usage of) the idea of 'liberty.'

Putting this all another way, the conclusion of our analysis was an hypothesis designed to explain actual usage. Like any other inductive hypothesis about something that actually happens, it was never a deductively necessary conclusion, but one that remained tentative and always subject to revision in the face of new evidence.

To explain tangible scenarios like plane crashes we look for underlying physical causes. To account for how we apply a concept or idea we look for underlying conceptual content—content which we can uncover by unpacking the idea. In our example, we came up with a sequence of conclusions, each an improvement over its predecessor and each subject to on-going correction, always guided by evidence.

But now, what was the evidence that guided our analysis? It came from three sources:

First, our data (the premises for our reasoning) were drawn from our acquaintance with the concept of 'liberty.' This was essentially our recognition of which "things" we were willing to say "fit" under that concept. Which societies, for example, would we call free?

The second source of information was our paradigm case. This is the representative example or model we were able to offer on the basis of our acquaintance with the concept of liberty and our background knowledge of existing societies. This representative instance of liberty served as a model which we could examine in order to come up with the components of our concept. In our example, they turned out to be majority rule together with an array of personal freedoms.

The third source was our counterexamples, one actual and one imagined. Recall that our evolving accounts or "definitions" of 'liberty' were always tentative and subject to the interdictions of these counterexamples which posed explanatory hurdles and therefore served as test cases for any results we had so far.

To sum up, the premises which essentially consisted of our findings about actual usage were explained by our conclusion which spelled out the meaning of "liberty" that would make the best fit with the evidence. Along the way, we entertained several possible analyses of our concept. These might be thought of as rival conclusions whose plausibilities were always subject to the "pressures" of some paradigm case and any available counterexamples.

Some writers are fond of telling a famous story about how a single counterexample can dramatically knock down a proposed analysis. The story is about a handful of students in ancient Athens doing philosophy at the time of Plato and Socrates. They were gathered one warm, Greek afternoon in a courtyard trying to hammer out a satisfactory analysis of the concept 'man.' When several of them began to settle on "featherless biped" as the desired "definition," a plucked chicken which someone threw over the wall landed at their feet. The eavesdropper had apparently followed the discussion closely and, it seems, would have been a star student in the group.

ONE SMALL WORRY
ABOUT PARADIGM CASES

You could, by now, be a bit troubled by what seems to be an element of circularity in the use of paradigm cases. After all, if we don't already know what socio-political liberty is, how can we select a good example of it, i.e., a paradigm case? And if we already know what it is, what need have we to define it?

The answer is straightforward enough. We know what liberty is only in a certain sense of "knowing"—the sense of acquaintance. We know when we have it and when we don't, which means we can recognize instances of it. Or, as we can also put it, we know how to apply the concept 'liberty' (or, what comes to the same thing, the term "liberty") to actual societies. And this is like knowing that someone loves you without being able to say what love is or by what clues you recognize it. Or again, it is like knowing that the speaker we're hearing is a good one without, at the moment, being able to say just what makes a good speaker.

This means we can single out a good example of what we want to characterize. We can then examine it for the characteristics which, on the basis of our general sophistication and background, we judge relevant to the concept in question, be it 'love,' 'oratory,' or 'liberty.' Paradigm cases therefore serve as models for guiding our analysis much like a model guides the painter or clues at the scene of a crime guide the investigator to a sense of what might have actually happened.

We should, however, pause here for some caution. We want to guard against a possible confusion of concept analysis—the kind of reasoning we have just discussed—with "analysis" in the sense in which it occurs in certain formal sciences and in mathematics (as, for example, algebra) where the thinking is unquestionably deductive rather than diagnostic.

Quite true, in algebraic analysis we also unpack something. Typically, this consists of "solving" an equation. Solving an equation itself, however, consists of manipulating it in strict accordance with clearly stipulated definitions and a set of rules whose deductive validity has already been soundly established. This guarantees that the operations we perform on the equation are deductively valid steps toward a solution. When we have solved the equation, therefore, what we have done is started with that equation as a premise and concluded with its solution (or solutions) as a necessary or deductively implied consequence of that equation and the rules by which we proceeded.

This is a different affair from what we're calling concept analysis. In dissecting a concept, we are dealing with the vagaries of a growing natural language and the corresponding conceptual frameworks that are changing and growing with that language. The meanings we seek, therefore, are not grounded in some fixed set of stipulations such as those in mathematics, which the mathematical community accepts by formal agreement. The meanings we try to unpack, instead, must be inferred inductively on the basis of what we can make out about current general usage. And we can do this only by examining representative examples of such usage.

Our conclusions, therefore, rather than being deductively necessary consequences of some set of premises are, instead, diagnostic—and therefore inductive—inferences. Alternative conclusions are always possible though hopefully less plausible than the one we decide to settle on. What is more, revisions are always in order as soon as compelling examples and counterexamples present themselves.

Concept analysis is, of course, largely an armchair activity. Its subject matter is abstract, consisting of concepts, impressions, recognitions, and dictionary entries—ordinarily requiring no laboratory or field work. It is perhaps this feature that has fostered an old mythology, namely, the misguided view that concept analysis is a purely deductive process. Admittedly, we do ordinarily associate induction, particularly of the diagnostic sort, almost exclusively with concrete happenings like crimes, accidents, and natural phenomena. But as our discussion has hopefully shown, the inductive mode of reasoning can operate even when the subject matter involved is not of this concrete, sensory sort.

＊　　＊　　＊

For now, let's put our concept scalpel aside and go to our next chapter, where we encounter another kind of concept processing—a kind which, in a sense, is the reverse of concept analysis and which we therefore refer to as *concept synthesis.*

20

SYNTHETICAL THINKING:
Creating a New Idea

THINKING SYNTHETICALLY

You have at one time or another dreamed up many ideas that were different in some interesting way from anything you had ever seen or thought of before—a golden mountain, a car that flies over traffic jams, a smart traffic light that responds to traffic density, a toll system without toll booths, a drink that can make you invisible. When you have done this you have created a new concept. The parts of your creation are themselves not new, but the combination is—at least as far as you are know. If it turns out that your new concept is in some important way unlike anything else that anyone has ever thought of and you publicize it, then you have contributed to our already immeasurable store of such *synthesized* concepts.

The building of concepts or concept synthesis, as we are calling it, is one of the most creative and wealth-producing kinds of thinking. Without it the existence (and progress) of our industrial, artistic, and scientific cultures is unimaginable. Even more than this, creative thinking is an immensely fulfilling activity. Any wonder, then, that concept building is so hugely prized in every area of human endeavor?

THE CREATIVITY IN CONCEPT SYNTHESIS

It is no great trick to throw concepts together whimsically and come up with novel combinations: blue monkeys, square oranges, mouse-sized elephants, and so on. In doing this we have only to be sure that the resulting concept is not self-contradictory as, for example, a square circle, four-sided triangle, or hairy reptile. (Reptiles are scaly, not hairy, by definition.) Contradictory expressions cannot be true of anything and consequently have no application or usage. In a sense, therefore, they do not correspond to any concepts at all.

Splicing concepts merely for the sake of novelty, however, is not the sort of synthesis that constitutes effective human creativity, even if we do it without contradicting ourselves. A machine can be easily programmed to lump ideas together blindly and endlessly. Creative concept building calls for much more. It occurs in a problem-solving context and is inventive, i.e., creative, rather than random. The problem may be an immediate one, like our having to wait needlessly for traffic lights to change when there is no cross traffic; or an imagined one, like dreaming up a lifeform that could survive far hotter temperatures than those on Earth; or a fantasy, like wishing you could become invisible any moment you want to. It may even be an artistic endeavor—an attempt to combine things (forms, colors, sounds, and so on) in a new and aesthetic way. In any case, the thinking is typically crafted to accomplish a specific task within some framework of interest.

When someone (perhaps da Vinci) first reflected on the importance of stealth in getting past a fleet of ships or even in approaching for an attack, he put together the novel concept of a seaworthy but submerged vessel: a submarine. Similarly, the composite idea of a vehicle which could move with inanimate power was synthesized in the context of the newly invented steam engine and a growing need for an untiring iron horse that could haul big loads over great distances.

The history of human invention offers us an endless stream of such examples. For some of the most spectacular leaps of concept synthesis, we need only look at our sciences. Here are only a few drawn from theoretical physics:

- Electron: A particle much smaller than an atom and too small to reflect light, so that it will never be directly visible, that carries a finite but indivisible amount of electric charge.

- Electric field: A chunk of space which even when otherwise "empty" can, at every point in it exert a force on an electrically charged particle.

- Neutrino: An electrically neutral particle with no measurable mass yet capable of absorbing and carrying off energy.

- Black hole: A place in space where the pull of gravity is so strong that it swallows up everything in its vicinity, including light.

- Quantum mechanical entity: An entity which can behave either as particle or wave depending on how we choose to observe it.

- Warped space: Space with geometric properties different from those of standard geometry.

Some of these concepts are so strange and counterintuitive that they defy our ability to form a clear mental image of the physical "things" they are supposed to correspond to. Yet, they work well within the theories that they were designed for, and in fact serve as key elements of these theories.

CONCEPT CREATION AS REASONING

Is the thinking that is involved in producing new concepts anything we can call reasoning? We get little or no help from logic and
reasoning textbooks on this question. The going wisdom has been
to insist, without much justification, that concept synthesis is a
nonreasoning process for which there can be no recipe or "logic."
It is simply the flash of insight, an irreducible creation. We are
especially good at it only when naturally gifted, though, admittedly, familiarity with the subject helps enormously.

Even granting all the novelty, spontaneity, and flash, the "no
reasoning" conclusion by no means follows. For one thing, the
thinking may be too fast and too hidden from full awareness for
its structure to be apparent at the time it occurs. Evidence that this
may sometimes be the case is the fact that very often we can
review an act of concept-building not merely for the usefulness or
other modes of "correctness" in the final idea, but also for the rea-
sonableness of whatever cognitive steps were taken to arrive at it.

There certainly are notable autobiographical accounts in
which authors reveal the reasoning strategies they used in
arriving at some new and wonderful idea. Often these are only
jump-start analogies sometimes followed by shades of diagnostic
reasoning. I cannot help recalling Albert Einstein's own vivid
account of how he first hit on the profoundly radical notion of
light having always the same velocity relative to any observer, no
matter how that observer herself might be moving.

Einstein imagined himself traveling at the speed of light
while holding a source of light—let's say, a flashlight—pointed
straight out, in the forward direction. He tells us what he thought
would happen in this make-believe situation. He and the searchlight would of course be moving forward at the very speed of the
emitted light itself. Despite all this, he imagined he would nevertheless observe that the light he was beaming would still shoot
straight ahead, piercing the darkness ahead of him and illuminating the space beyond. Another way of putting this is to say
that Einstein and the searchlight would never catch up to the light

beam the way a supersonic projectile catches up with and sur-
passes the very sound it produces.

Einstein was of course drawing analogies from his familiarity with a light beam in ordinary situations. The analogy did
stretch things a bit because of the almost grotesquely strange
nature of his imagined (*gedanken*) experiment. It was reasoning,
nonetheless; it was reasoning of the analogical and therefore
inductive sort. His conclusion had diagnostic undertones
explaining what he imagined he would observe.

Sometimes the reasoning is tighter as, for example, in G. J.
Stoney's concept of an indivisible grain of electricity, i.e., the
electron. The thinking in this case involved him in an analogy
with the atom and in some very neat diagnostic reasoning about
a whole array of careful measurements that Michael Faraday had
made half a century earlier.

For a still more concrete example, let's go back to ancient
architecture: Basic to all structural engineering in ancient Greece
was the straight beam which rested on two opposed walls and
spanned the distance between them to support weight on a floor
or a roof. The strength of this beam depended on its resistance to
bending, especially at the center of the span. We still use such a
beam today much as the Greeks did millennia ago. The Greeks,
however, did not have our steel beams. They used wood whose
strength was of course severely limited and fell short of what was
needed for loads and spans that were very large, as in the case of
aqueducts, bridges, and some public buildings.

To meet this need, the Romans created a new idea: the arch.
It was a synthesis of two familiar concepts: the straight line distance to be spanned and the curvature of the arch that would span
that distance. The arch, essentially an upwardly humped or
curved beam, was able to do what was utterly undreamed of with
a straight-line beam.

Now, how could these ancient architects have come up with
such an idea? As in any problem solving, some blind groping and
free association followed by simple trial and error was no doubt
involved. Our concern, however, is with whatever processes

might have occurred in guiding the thinking toward the final idea.

The first factor that comes to mind here is the role of background knowledge in the creation of a new idea. (Even those who regard creative thinking as "pure revelation" concede that it is usually the sophisticated insiders with the requisite knowledge that are most productive.) At any rate, our ancient architects could have reasoned in the following way: A sagged beam is very analogous to an arch; it is an upside-down arch. What if we started with a rightside-up arch instead of a straight beam? We could then hope that, under the expected load, we would end up with a straight beam, i.e., a beam without sag. This is inductive reasoning of a crudely analogical sort, along with some expectation of symmetry (reversibility) in the behavior of the beam—all based on some vague experiences of the past.

Now, in order for our arch to sag, its ends must spread apart. This follows deductively from the geometry involved. As the upwardly arched beam sags, it must spread out and therefore span a greater horizontal distance than it did before.

Eureka! If we secure the ends of the arch, so that they could not be moved outwardly, it would be mathematically (deductively) impossible for the arch to sag—provided of course that the material of which it is made does not crush and collapse under the resulting compression. This is unlikely because (as the ancients must have known), solids are generally far more resistant to compression than to bending. Fine, the two ends could, therefore, be jammed between the two opposing sides of a gully or between two firm structures.

By arching their beams, these architects, it seems, cleverly and deliberately converted bending (for straight beams) into compression (for arched ones). So complete was this transformation that they could now sometimes dispense with a solid continuous beam altogether. The new arched "beam" or simply the arch could now be constructed out of individual segments such as stones and bricks, properly angled to produce the desired arch and rigidity.

The arch can indeed be seen as a truly creative bit of concept synthesis. It was certainly a novel idea, though others before had certainly seen a camel's back or the arched ceiling of a natural cave. Moreover, it was an architectural triumph and would no doubt still rank supreme today if not for the advent of the straight steel beam of unprecedented strength and relative lightness.

How the idea *actually* bubbled up, we'll probably never know. By imagining how it might have taken shape, however, we have established at least the possibility of a structured process in the thinking that took place. If our reconstruction is anywhere near correct, the full conceptualization of the Roman arch most certainly involved reasoning—reasoning *par excellence.* The reasoning must have been a web of both deductively and inductively guided thought ranging from crude analogies to more complicated predictions—spontaneously inspired though it may have seemed at the time.

Even in creating art, where thinking seems to be far less structured than in science or technology, reasoned judgment may play significant roles. Poets and painters speak of an idea as working or not working, fitting or not fitting, within the particular piece they are crafting. In claims of this sort, the suggestion is strong that an element of reasoned, predictive judgment is involved—that it operates in molding the artistic idea, possibly even in the very first act of conceiving it. Will the lonely, misty greys of both the sea water and the steep escarpment do the trick? Will the combination express the desolation I am depicting, and how will it be grasped by my viewers? The thinking could well be very fast, consisting of touch-and-go bits of reasoning, guided inductively with analogies and even some simple predictions based on past impressions.

A PSYCHOLOGICAL MATTER

A complex idea like a structural arch could of course pop into anyone's head at any time. The question of how this is most likely to happen, however, is a matter more for psychologists or even neuroscientists than it is for students of the logic in reasoning. One can, for example, imagine any number of triggers for an idea like an arched beam: a dream, a free association, even a delusion. Indeed, neuroscientists are now offering studies showing that conscious intuitions and hunches have a firm biological basis in unconsciously stored "emotional memories."*

Still, this is not inconsistent with a trace of reasoning, possibly only a weak analogy, lighting up the way at the start of the process. Once the "first flash" has occurred, though, the concept processing that can follow is quite another matter. When our ancient architects finally matched their novel idea to the problematic context in which they found themselves, they had to reason, no matter how spontaneously and rapidly.

❋   ❋   ❋

Having introduced the unpacking and "packing" of concepts, let us now go to our final chapter on concepts. There we take up three crucially important cognitive activities which make use of these processes. The first of these, *abstraction,* is absolutely essential in the sense that without it, coherent discourse as we know it would be impossible. The second, *explication,* is the big player in those areas where specialized study or decision making or communication require us to be more precise with language. The third, *distinction making,* has to do with what we might call concept-vision. It is a basic mental skill which is hardly ever discussed anywhere, but which measures our capacity for at least one kind of intelligence—namely, high-resolution thinking.

---

*New York Times, March 4, 1997, p. C5.

21

RESECTING, RESHAPING, AND DIFFERENTIATING CONCEPTUAL TISSUE

ABSTRACTION

Without abstractions communication would be little more than a series of reciprocal grunts and gestures. Sentences, arguments, and communicable reasoning would be unheard of; words would be little more than attention-getting sounds and pointings to concrete objects. The very moment we refer to a class of things— man, mouse, muffin—we are using an abstraction. What we understand by nearly all our words (i.e., the concepts that constitute their meanings) are abstractions, whose degree or level we can change by a kind of concept-processing that goes by the same name as the product itself, namely, abstraction.

The process of abstraction is closely related to concept analysis. Instead of unpacking an entire idea, however, in abstraction, we single out and delete only a portion of it. What remains is said to be a more abstract concept than the original. A house is a building that serves as living quarters. If we delete from the concept 'house' the part about living quarters, we are left with a more abstract concept, namely, 'building.'

We can take any concept and trim it more and more so as to make it more and more abstract for whatever application we have in mind. If for example, we cut out the idea of 'enclosure' from the concept of 'building,' we get the more abstract concept of 'structure,' without specification as to whether it is a building, a bridge, a monument, and so on.

THE AWESOME POWER OF ABSTRACTIONS

Scientific theory is full of concepts that are very highly abstract. Some of these are remarkably simple. Here are a few familiar ones:

- Molecule: A particle having mass, location, and structure but invisible in all ordinary senses of "visible."

- Ideal market: A market in which prices respond instantly and strictly to supply and demand, and which therefore does not have the "inertia" of actually existing markets.

- Ideal business manager: A manager who, unlike real managers, acts *always* for maximizing profits and not out of other drives or intellectual failure.

- Ideal gas: A gas which, unlike real gases, consists of molecules that are completely elastic and therefore do not dissipate energy when they bump into each other and that have no attraction whatever for each other.

- Frictionless plane: A flat surface that offers absolutely no resistance to motion.

In all but the first of these examples, the abstractions are also idealizations. That is, the deletions take the concepts right out of the realm of reality, because, strictly speaking, there are no such ideal entities. Such idealizations apply to real things only with approximation, but they afford tremendous simplification in the reasoning they make possible.

The usefulness and power of abstractions is immense and derives mainly from their generality which enables us to talk sweepingly (i.e., generally) about many things at once. By deleting more and more properties from some concept, we put fewer and fewer restrictions on the objects to which it applies; that is, we make the concept broader in its application—which of course means that it can be used to apply to a wider and wider range of things.

Generally, there are more houses in the world than there are English Tudors, more buildings than there are houses, more structures than there are buildings, and so on. Similarly, there are more (human) adults than there are women, more humans than there are adults, more primates than there are humans, more mammals than there are primates, more vertebrates than there are mammals, and so on up the ladder of abstraction. The conceptual content of our theoretical sciences is very abstract or general because these sciences attempt to give accounts of vast stretches of subject matter at once.

ABSTRACTIONS ARE ELUSIVE

Though concepts become more and more sweeping and powerful as we make them more and more abstract, they also become more elusive and difficult to handle. The reason is that, as we excise content from a concept, it becomes harder for us to visualize or otherwise imagine whatever remains of the now rarefied concept. Abstracting eventually deletes content associated with concrete properties like shape, color, texture, smell, and so on, and so we loose touch, as it were, with the solid sensory props that ordinarily guide our thinking.

In the process of abstracting, we can lop off attributes to the point where all that is left is just one general attribute, e.g., color (in general), texture (in general), quantity (in general), or shape (in general). The late nineteenth-century French impressionists illustrated this process aesthetically by making the property of color and the play of light that produced color effects the essential subject matter of their paintings. Later, some artists like Franz Kline (1910–1962) or Mark Rothko (1903–1970) presented a brush stroke or even just a block of color on a canvas.

The concepts—color, texture, quantity, etc.—resulting from such drastic abstraction will, of course, be exceedingly general. Nevertheless, if they are shared in some important way by enough "things," they can become the subject matter of entire areas of study. Monumental examples of such elemental concepts are 'quantity' and 'geometric shape,' the subjects of a major chunk of our intellectual heritage, namely, mathematics.

Rarefied abstractions of this sort are characteristic of many of the theoretical sciences which, for this reason, most of us consider intellectually demanding. Add to this that it often becomes necessary to introduce unfamiliar language (symbols, new words, cryptic labels, etc.) for new abstractions and these subjects can become really intimidating. Just remembering (never mind picturing) what the symbols refer to can be fatally daunting to anyone but the trained specialist.

At any rate, for the purposes of both thinking and communicating it is crucially important to be cautious with highly abstract concepts, no matter what the subjects involved are. Scrupulous reference to examples, illustrative models, and concrete applications is highly recommendable if not entirely indispensable. In this general regard, we might paraphrase something the philosopher Immanuel Kant said in one of his most seminal works: "Percepts without concepts are blind; concepts without percepts are empty."

This whole subject reminds me of some desolating experiences as a graduate student at Princeton where the physics department was heavily inclined toward theory. Humble rookies that we were, we suffered in silence. We languished for concrete examples as each of the European-styled lecturers elaborated his particular branch of mathematical physics by stacking concept upon concept in an ever-swelling sea of ghostly abstractions.

Coming out of the numbing cold on a winter morning and then sitting in the embracing warmth of an old gothic classroom in Palmer Hall, the abstractions became pure chloroform. On really cold mornings, in our analytical mechanics class, where the professor lectured in broken Norwegian (broken English would have been a godsend), I was never able to count beyond twenty-six before losing active consciousness.

The half-dozen or so of us never got to compare notes on our resistance to these lethargizing influences, but it was evident that we were all thirsting for the rarest of treats in those days, namely, a solid application of the endless theory. When an all-too-brief example finally came, it was like getting a heartbeat under CPR. You could sense the tension release as some color returned both to the abstractions and to us as well.

CONCEPT SHARPENING: Analysis + Synthesis

LOVE(?)

Nearly all of us, I'm sure, have heard someone say "I love you," and wondered what to make of it. Did the speaker really mean it? Or was he being carried away by the moment or merely being nice? Even when firmly convinced of another's sincerity and seriousness, we might still have some gnawing doubts about what he actually intends by such a declaration—and with good reason. The word "love" is used so variously and, to make matters worse, so vaguely, that no matter how close our attention, we can be at sea about the meaning of what we're hearing. I've heard my wife say "love you" even just to thank a benefactor she hardly knew.

Of course, semantic obsession of this sort could dampen any romance, but certainly there are times when we really "must" understand what a declaration of love amounts to. We may want to predict another's conduct, or take a reasonable position in a marital issue, or else, simply know where we stand at some critical point in a relationship. In such intimate circumstances, paying close attention to context and to other aspects of communication (body language, tone, etc.) seems to be about the best we can do to avoid deception or error.

There are, however, very special contexts—legal, psychological, commercial, moral, or literary—in which a clearer concept of even something as personal and subjective as love, would be great to have. For the technical purposes that can arise in such contexts, ordinary usage, as we find it, is much too vague, though it is all we usually have to go by.

THE WAY TO GO: Explication

A reasonable way to go is to do some concept sharpening or explication. This may seem like a desperate measure but we resort to it often. It amounts to refining and clarifying ordinary usage for the purposes we have in mind. In doing this, we, of course, do not want to break too radically from what a key word ordinarily means. Such a thing would do intolerable violence to what we already vaguely understand by the corresponding concept. Our task instead is largely one of adjustment.

EXPLICATING THE CONCEPT OF LOVE

To help flesh out our reflections so far, let's try something outrageous—a brief explication of the concept of 'love.' In a book on something as "cool" as reasoning, doing this for something as "warm" as love may seem freakish if not plain silly. (It is arcane notions like 'probability' or 'reasonable doubt' that are generally regarded as calling for explication.) The intimate familiarity most of us have with the concept of 'love' makes it a good choice for illustrative purposes.

For simplicity, let's restrict ourselves to romantic love and begin with a definition based on a dictionary entry for the word "love"—which, of course, reports current usage. Let's start by saying that "I love you" means "I have a strong and sympathetic interest in you, together with admiration and a desire to be with you." This definition is essentially a start-up analysis or "unpacking" of the concept of 'love' as we find it in current usage.

Now, imagine that the contexts we have in mind are demanding and require us to be more specific on what we mean by the word "sympathetic." In such a case, what we're after obviously calls for a prescriptive portion that tells us how the term "love" *should* be used if it is to be effective in the work that we have in mind for it. Refining—perhaps better, redefining—the concept in this way means not only spelling out (analyzing) and utilizing how it is used in ordinary discourse, but also "rebuilding" it with a bit of the sort of concept processing we have called concept synthesis.

Okay then, we can add that a lover must be willing to make a few serious commitments—even at high material cost. One of these could be to engage in a lifetime of intimate sharing and exclusive cohabitation. Another might be to promote mutual growth and personal fulfillment. And we may also remember that intimacy calls forth still other conditions: confidentiality, loyalty, faith. We might even want to go further and add something about mutual respect, mutual regard for personal space, equality, and individual autonomy.

This has been, of course, a purely hypothetical or makebelieve explication of love, intended not by any means to "standardize" our conception of it but only to illustrate explication as a type of concept processing.

In attempting to arrive at our result the idea was twofold. First; we wanted a concept of 'love' which makes a good fit with all that we know about what we vaguely and uncritically refer to as "love." Second, we wanted a concept which was refurbished and refined to a degree of explicit richness and precision well beyond its vague day-to-day version. The idea was not to remake our perfectly natural and given experience of love. Rather, it was to frame or explicate a concept that would be more suitable in some special area of human affairs. Our explication once implemented by those concerned in the relevant contexts could conceivably do this. It could, for example, enable us to predict and better understand (perhaps even clinically) the behavior of someone who, in those contexts, declares her or his love for another. Also, it could help demarcate, in certain social and legal contexts, any obligations freely assumed by someone making the declaration. Of course, the usefulness of our modified concept depends on the fit it makes with the realities of the intended domain of application.

Our everyday concepts are fuzzy, and this is fine for most purposes. But even in ordinary conversations we sometimes feel an immediate urge to explicate a concept in order to establish a point. When this happens, just go ahead. We are remarkably good at rough and ready explications. Try it on such juicy subjects as beauty, aesthetic merit, friendship, freedom, or responsibility.

PHILOSOPHICAL EXPLICATION

Some philosophers tell us that explication is central to all philosophizing and perhaps even constitutes the bulk of it. Even if they are only partially right, our natural penchant for this kind of activity makes us all, at least in this regard, incurably philosophical. Recall the spiritedness and pleasure of some discussions you had whenever the subject was ideas. A good number of these discussions were probably instances of concept-refining or rebuilding—the very process we are calling *explication*.

SCIENTIFIC EXPLICATION

In science, explication is more than a gratuitous leisurely activity. It is often the crucial step in the formulation of theories. The process takes theorists from familiar prescientific terms to retailored meanings that will fit their theoretical frameworks better than the parent meanings. The resulting concepts then typically become essential parts of the theories for which they were designed.

Illustrations of explication are easily pulled from the pages of our theoretical sciences. Physicists, for example, define "work" not loosely as any kind of effort or accomplishment but precisely and innovatively as a certain kind of mathematical product of force and distance. In certain branches of study, some researchers often construe the probability of an event not in the vague everyday sense of subjective uncertainty, but in terms of the relative frequency with which that event has occurred in the past. Chemists define a term like "gold" not by color, density, hardness, or even its resistance to nearly all acids, but precisely by the number of protons in the atomic nuclei of the corresponding substance. Zoologists define "fish" not roughly by how much time the corresponding organism spends in water, but by its biological structure. And this list can be extended on and on to include terms like "inertia," "momentum," "power," "acid," "money," and much more.

Finally, we should mention that some authors regard an explication as a kind of definition—sometimes referring to it as a theoretical or explicative definition. And indeed, when we have modified a concept or meaning by explicating it we have in a very real sense "defined" the corresponding term or, perhaps better, redefined it. We prefer to call the process explication, however, simply to underline the fact that it is a form of concept processing, which is neither analysis nor synthesis alone but a combination of both.

DISTINCTION MAKING:
A Signature of Smartness

INTELLIGENCE(?)

I once asked my teacher, the late Sidney Hook—educator, philosopher, and critic—what he meant by "intelligence." His answer was "The ability to make inferences." The answer then seemed quite natural and convincing. Of course the activity he was referring to was nothing other than what we are here calling reasoning. Some time later however, I heard a very different but equally appealing definition of intelligence, this time from a literary critic who said that intelligence was the ability to make distinctions. He was referring, of course, to distinguishing one shade of meaning or nuance from another or equivalently, one concept from another, closely similar one.

Since those early days, I've heard a good many other one-liners on intelligence. Some link it to other abilities like that of making good decisions, setting priorities correctly, focussing on essentials, retaining information, or getting along with fellow humans. Others point to creativity, insightfulness, flexibility, and even moral sense. Psychologists today seem to prefer speaking of many kinds of intelligence or cognitive ability rather than of any sort of "basal intelligence." The going view seems to be that those who try to fix on a "best" or most basic indicator of human intellectual power are engaging in a vain over-simplification— narrowly inspired by their own interests. Still, there seems to be something in the literary critic's reference to distinction making —something possibly as plausible as Hook's reference to inference making. For certainly, perceiving a shade of difference between two very similar meanings can be an illuminating and impressive mental feat.

CONCEPT PERCEPTION

Conceptual distinctions are usually first made as immediate perceptions very much like the sensory distinctions we make with our sight, taste, touch, hearing, etc. We readily distinguish between freedom and license or between humility and humbleness or between courage and recklessness much as we do between pink and coral or between firmness and hardness. And we tend to think those who make fine conceptual distinctions are

sharp of the mind, just as we think those who make fine percep-
tual distinctions are sharp of the senses. Furthermore, the greater
the power to "resolve" meanings, the keener we regard the minds
that have it. Conversely, we regard poor distinction making as
coarseness or obtuseness or "low resolution" thinking.

Imagine, for example, some counselor cautioning us to seek
justice, not revenge; to cultivate sentiment, not sentimentality; to
separate bigotry from mere insensitivity; or to be courteous not
obsequious, assertive not rude, firm not obstinate. Could we have
much doubt about her mental acuity?

DISTINCTION MAKING AND REASONING

Now, is distinction making reasoning? That is, is it the kind of
thinking which takes us from a set of premises to a conclusion?
Thinking which, like some diagnostic reasoning, is so rapid that
we lose sight of its structure? Or is it some sort of immediate
cognition, by which we simply understand or "see" that two similar concepts (meanings) are not quite the same? Opinion on this
matter remains divided.

The issue seems to be little more than academic in light of the
fact that once we have drawn a distinction between two very similar concepts, we can always test it to see if it holds up under
review. This review process is much more easily recognized as
reasoning than is the original "perception." Does making a distinction between courage and recklessness or between love and
infatuation work in actual discourse? Can we give instances
which we would call courageous but not reckless—or reckless
but not courageous?

Once I've made a distinction, there are reasons I can call up
to justify it. The reasons (premises, data) are whatever I can
remember about how the concepts involved actually apply to
concrete instances. Indeed, to cinch my argument, I may produce
concrete examples of distinguishable cases. At any rate, my conclusion is that the concepts I am "perceiving" as different are in

fact different. The review process, therefore, is an argument whose conclusion is that the two concepts are actually different and whose premises cite my original perception of a difference along with concrete examples illustrating the difference. The reasoning is inductive, and it takes us from our initial perception, plus distinguishable instances in actual discourse to a generalization that all such instances are similarly distinguishable—or, what is equivalent—to the basic or underlying difference we are claiming between the concepts involved. The reasoning is therefore diagnostic. Its conclusion explains our experience and this includes not only application of the concepts to particular instances but also our initial perception that the two concepts are different.

The central role of distinction making in much of our thinking makes exercising and cultivating it highly worthwhile. The going issue of how immediate or "intuitive" the thinking involved is may be unsettled, but it certainly seems advisable to put our flash judgments about closely similar concepts to some sort of reasoned test or review. The importance of doing such a review leaves reasoning as a major player in the exercise of even *this* human talent.

✳   ✳   ✳

And now, dear reader, we must say goodbye. You've inspired me as did Francesca when she popped into my office that late Friday afternoon and sparked my writing. It is you, though, who stayed the distance through entrancing and sometimes bemusing byways in a land long hidden from all but the insiders. Together we scanned the kinds of thinking we do when we try to justify our beliefs, explain what confronts us, and untangle the riddles in our lives. We formulated the right questions to ask fellow reasoners, pinpointed the boobytraps that can derail any of us, and planted flags to help us through the mined terrain. Finally, we tried our hand at some surgery—concept surgery. Our subjects were ideas instead of bodies, and for scalpels we had our wits. The anesthetics that eased the way were the satisfactions and the endorphins produced by our thinking.

I hope the trip has been as intimate and interactive for you as it has for me. It has helped me get clear on many points. I'll miss the warm comfort of your company as I wrote late into the night, and the excitement as we cut through some underbrush or managed to stay in flight, even when the air got a little thin. You alone will know the difference our experience together has made for you. If I, too, could know, I would judge the success of this book not so much by how many copies are sold but by the measure of this difference—your closer intimacy with the simplicity, beauty, and wondrous power of how we reason.

There's no need to remember details. We can always stay in touch. Just keep me as close as the nearest bookshelf.

INDEX